Fender

SPECIAL EDITION

JIMI HENDRIX EXPERIENCE
SMASH HITS

G-DEC 3

GUITAR DIGITAL ENTERTAINMENT CENTER

ISBN 978-1-4584-0089-5

HAL•LEONARD®
CORPORATION

7777 W. BLUEMOUND RD. P.O. BOX 13819 MILWAUKEE, WI 53213

Visit Hal Leonard Online at
www.halleonard.com

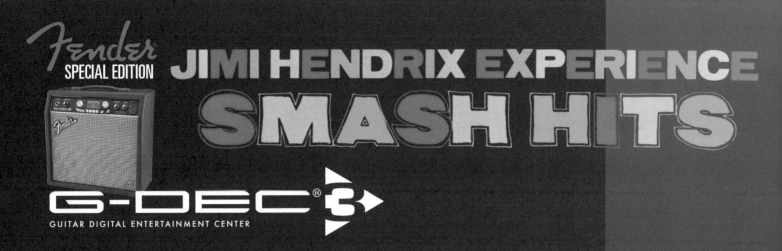

CONTENTS

Purple Haze

Words and Music by Jimi Hendrix

Intro
Moderate Rock ♩ = 106

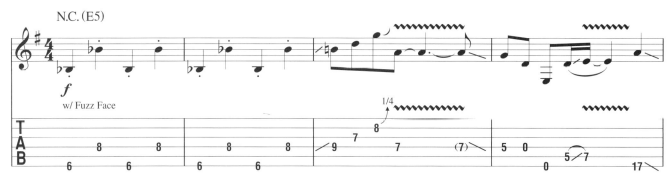

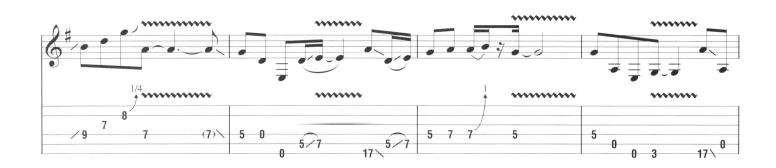

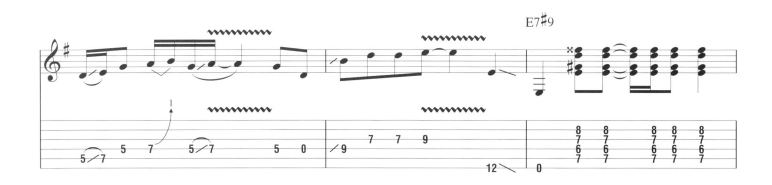

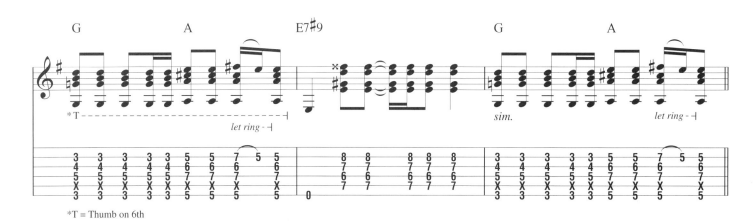

*T = Thumb on 6th

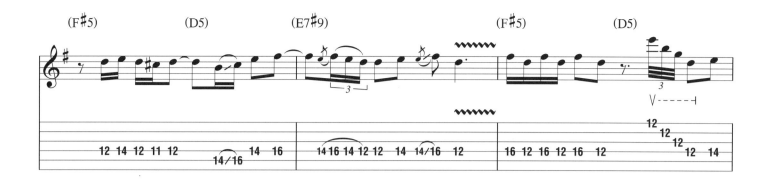

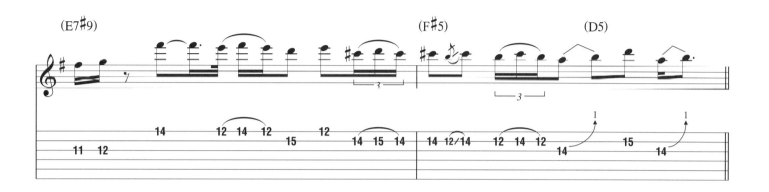

Interlude

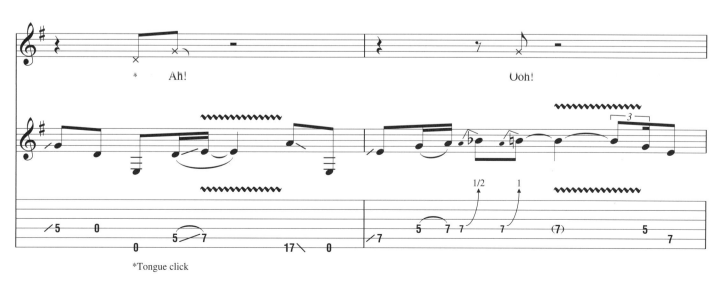

*Tongue click

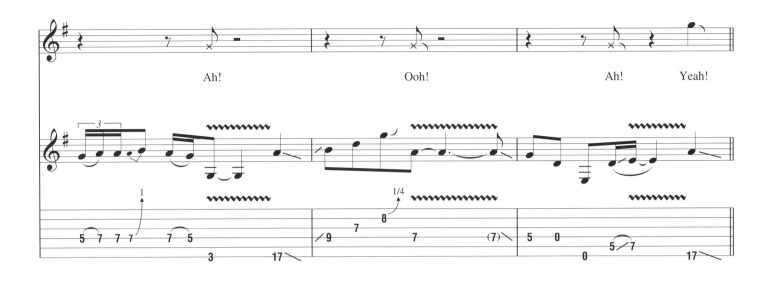

Ah! Ooh! Ah! Yeah!

Verse

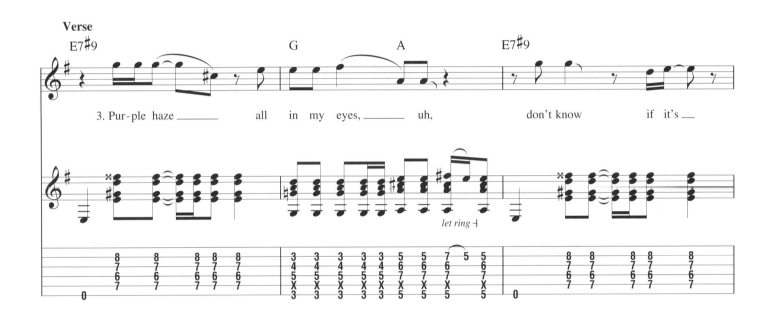

3. Pur-ple haze _____ all in my eyes, _____ uh, _____ don't know _____ if it's _____

let ring

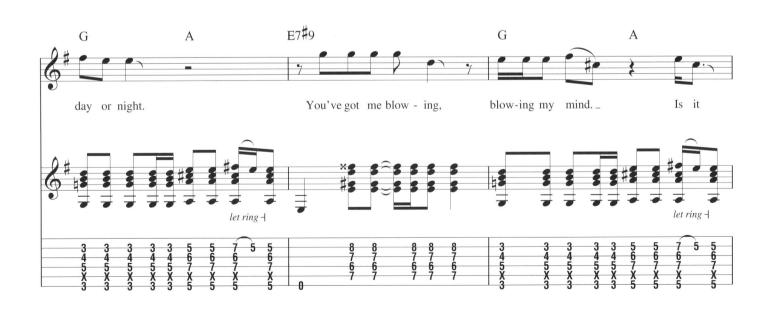

day or night. You've got me blow - ing, blow-ing my mind. _ Is it

let ring   _let ring_

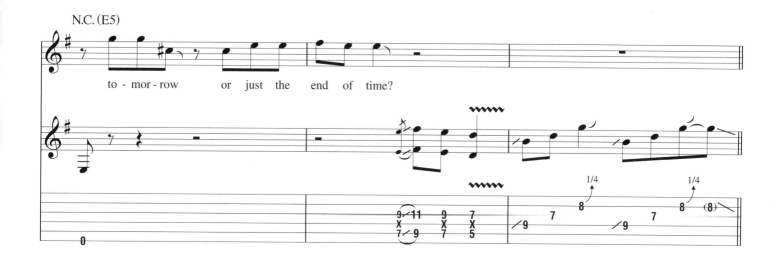

to - mor - row   or just the end of time?

Outro

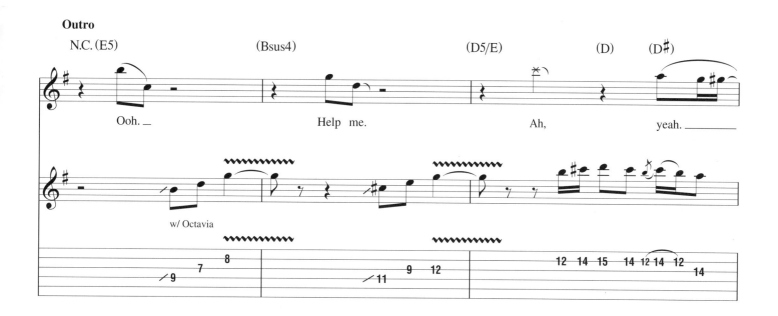

Ooh. __   Help me.   Ah,   yeah. _____

w/ Octavia

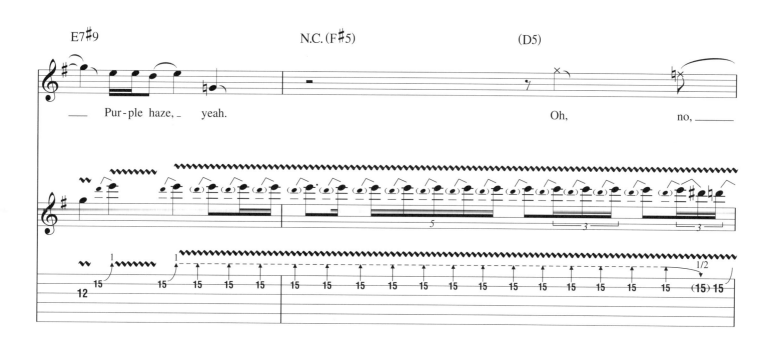

__ Pur - ple haze, _ yeah.   Oh,   no, _____

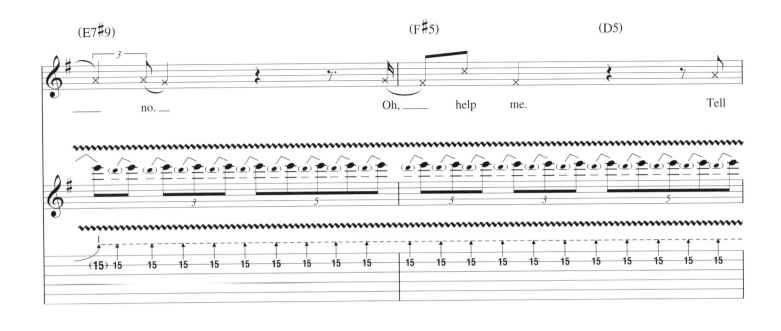

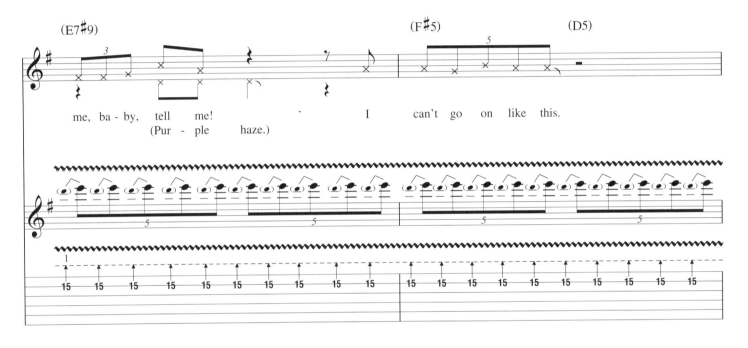

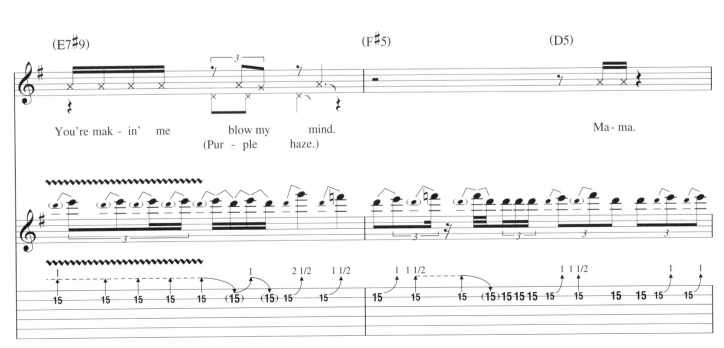

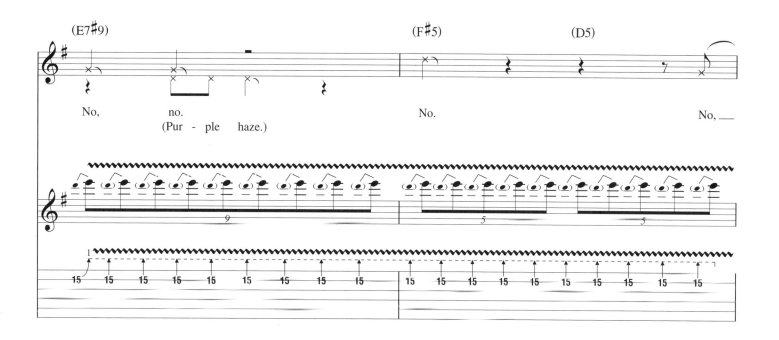

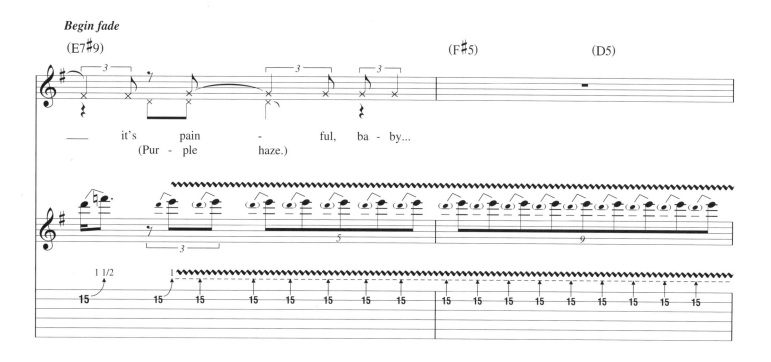

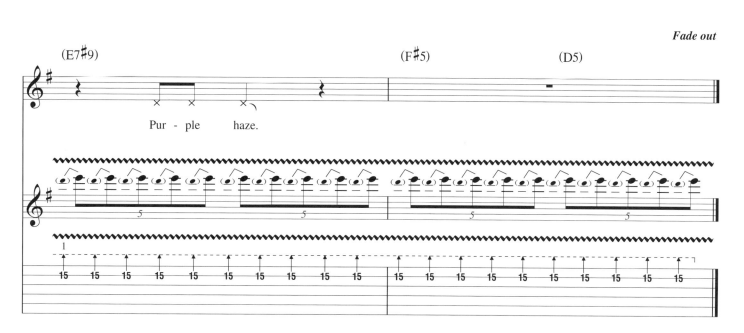

Fire

Words and Music by Jimi Hendrix

like it like _ that. I have _ on - ly one a burn - ing de - sire, ____

Chorus
Dadd9   Cadd9

let me stand _ next to your fire! _   Hey!
(Let me   stand _ next to your

*T = Thumb on 6th string.

Dadd9   Cadd9

Let me stand _ next to your fire!   Whoa, _ let me   stand, _
fire! _   Let me   stand _ next to your fire! _____

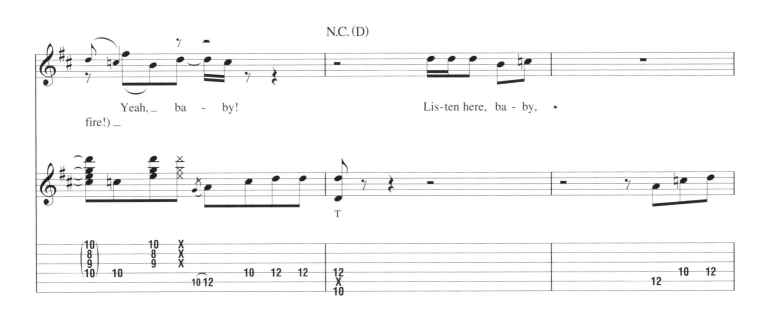

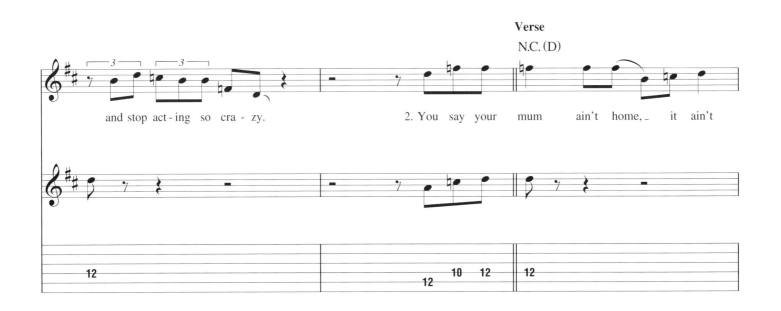

my con - cern. ___ Just a play with me and you won't get burned.

I have on - ly one a itch - ing de - sire, _____ *Spoken:* let me stand ___ next to your

Chorus

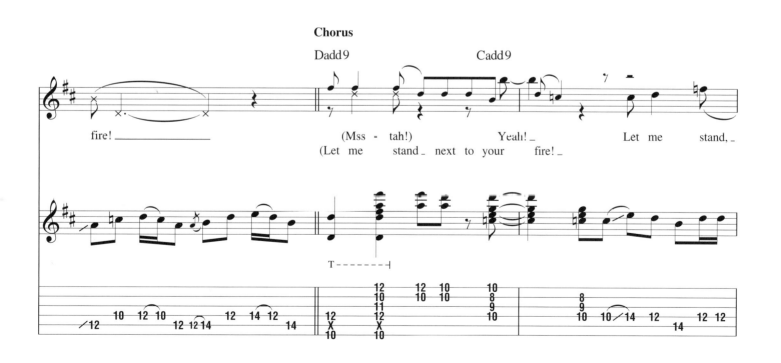

fire! _____ (Mss - tah!) Yeah! _ Let me stand, _
(Let me stand _ next to your fire! _

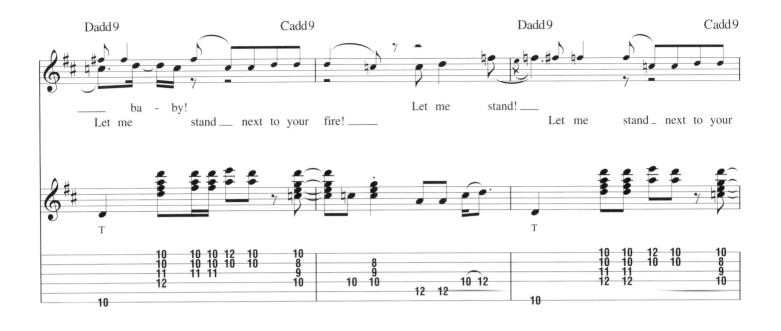

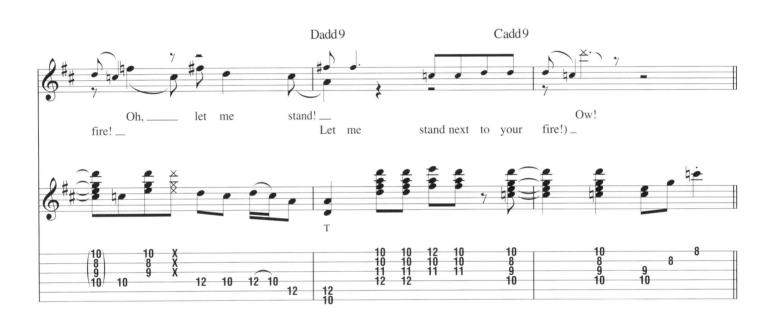

Bridge

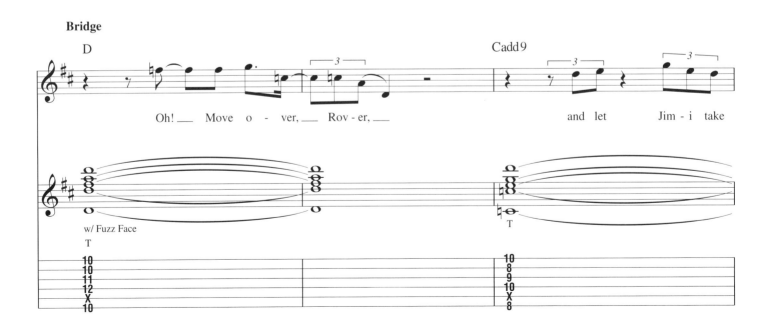

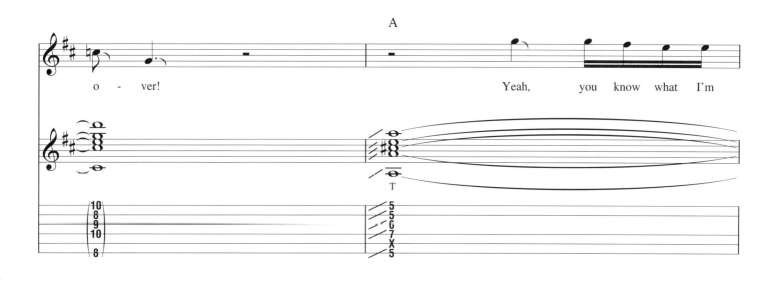

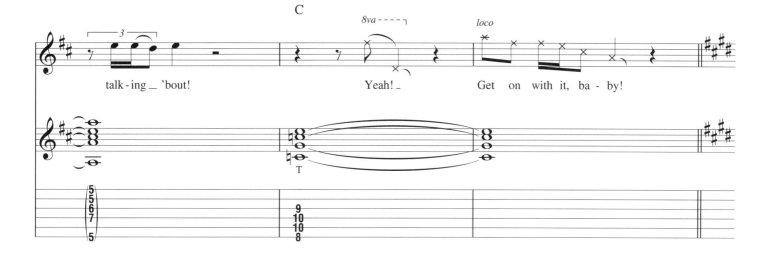

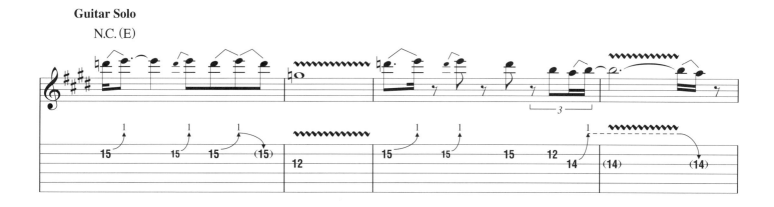

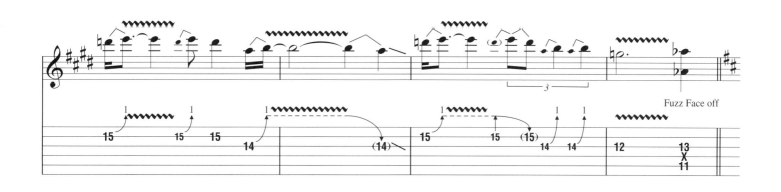

Interlude

N.C.

That's what I'm talk-ing 'bout. _

(D)

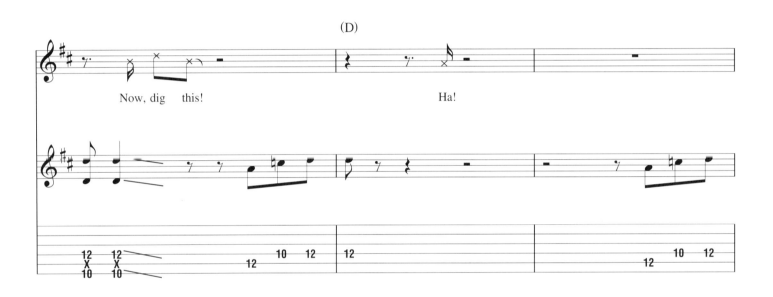

Now, dig this!   Ha!

Verse

N.C. (D)

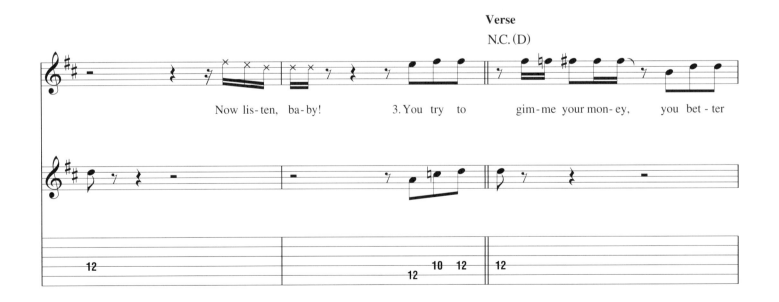

Now lis-ten, ba-by!   3. You try to   gim-me your mon-ey,   you bet-ter

save it, babe,   save it for ___ your ___ rain - y day. __

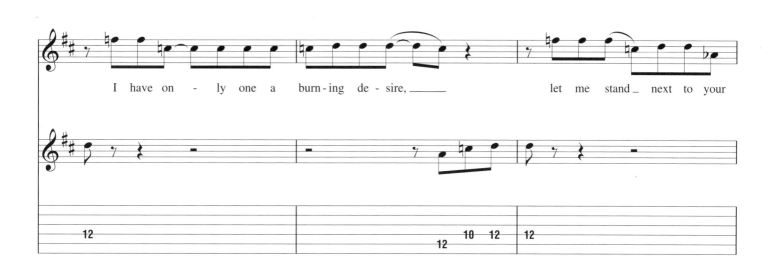

I have on - ly one a burn - ing de - sire, _____ let me stand _ next to your

Chorus

Dadd9   Cadd9

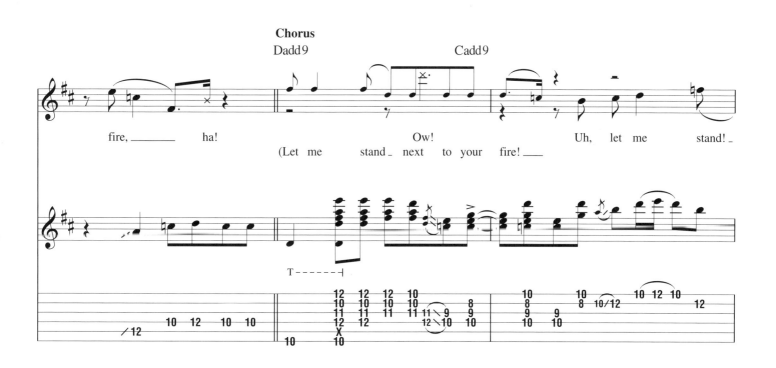

fire, _____ ha!   Ow!   Uh, let me   stand! _

(Let me stand _ next to your fire! ___

Outro

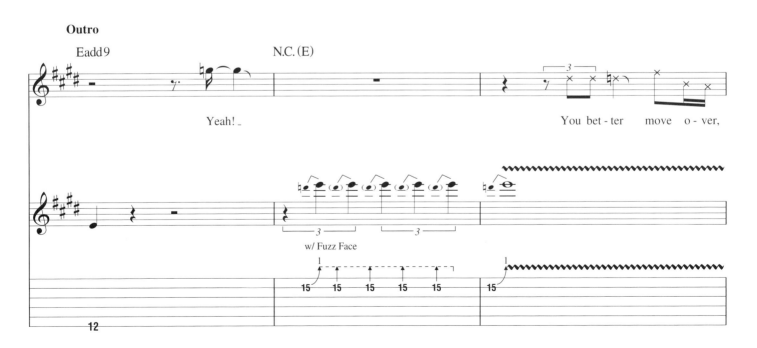

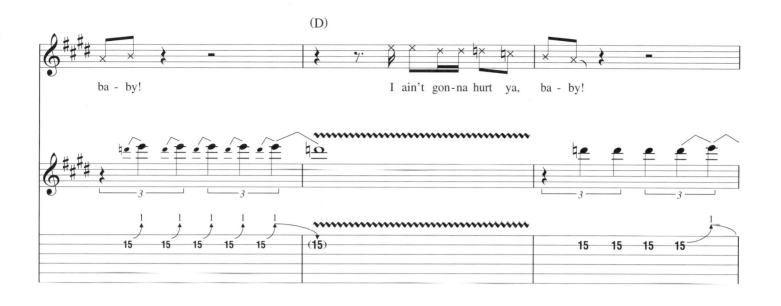

ba - by!   I ain't gon-na hurt ya,   ba - by!

Ah, ___   I ain't talk with your   ol' la - dy.   Ow!

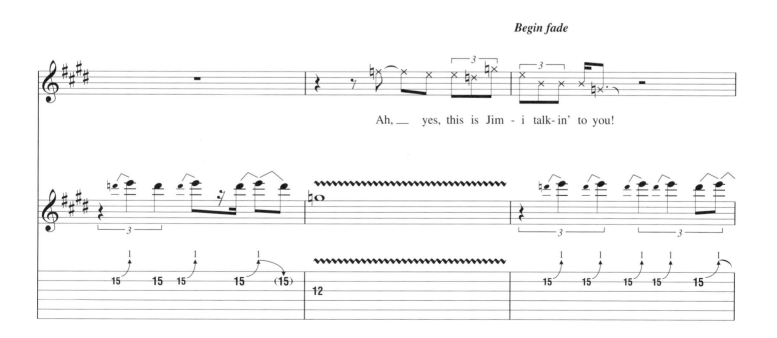

Begin fade

Ah, ___   yes, this is Jim - i talk-in' to you!

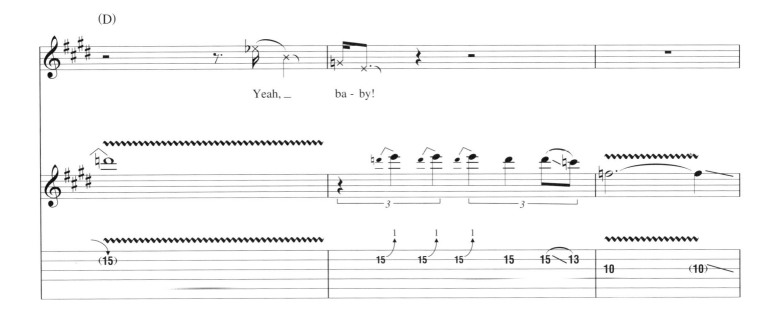

Yeah, __ ba - by!

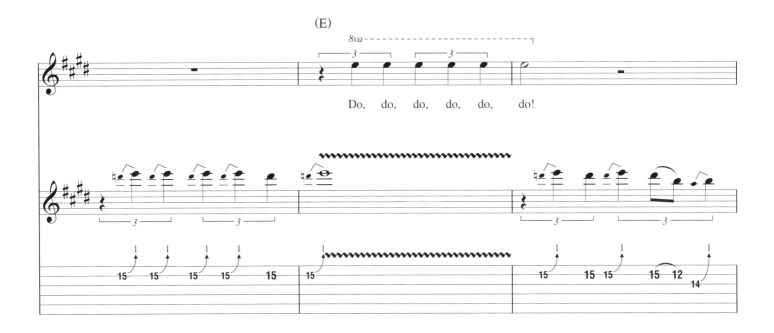

Do, do, do, do, do, do!

Fade out

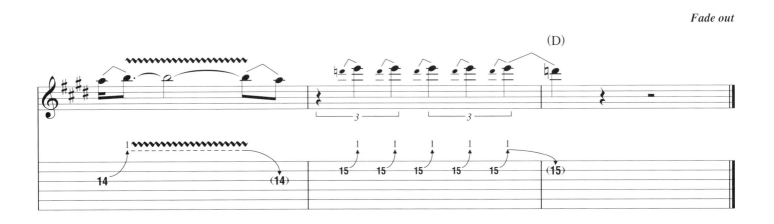

The Wind Cries Mary

Words and Music by Jimi Hendrix

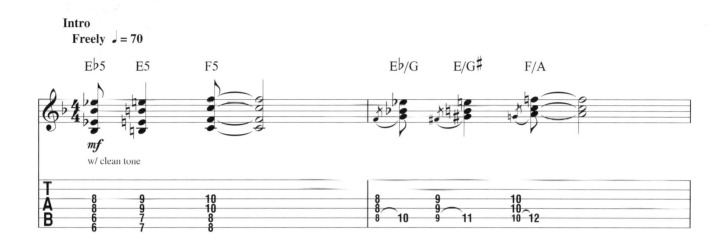

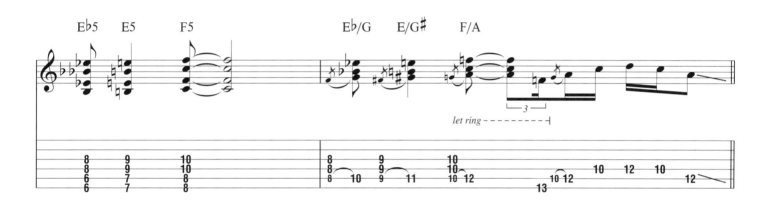

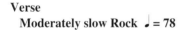

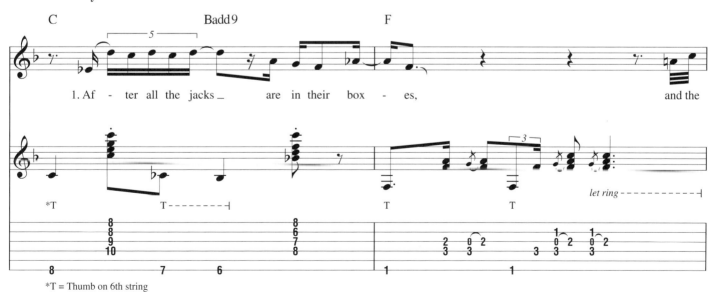

*T = Thumb on 6th string

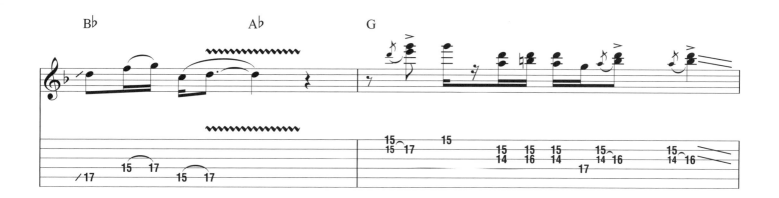

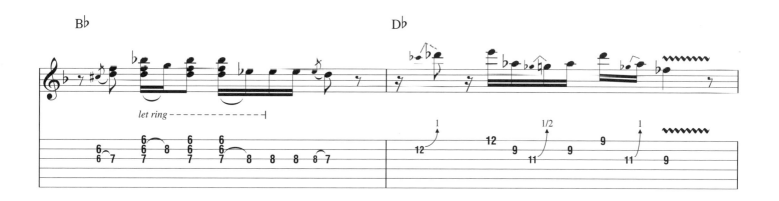

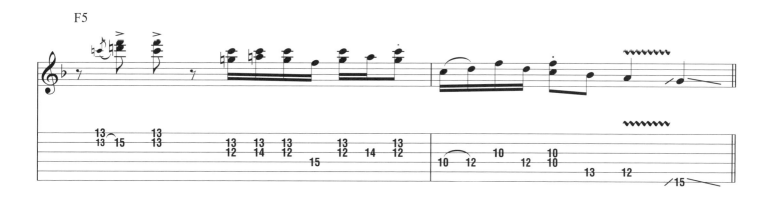

Verse

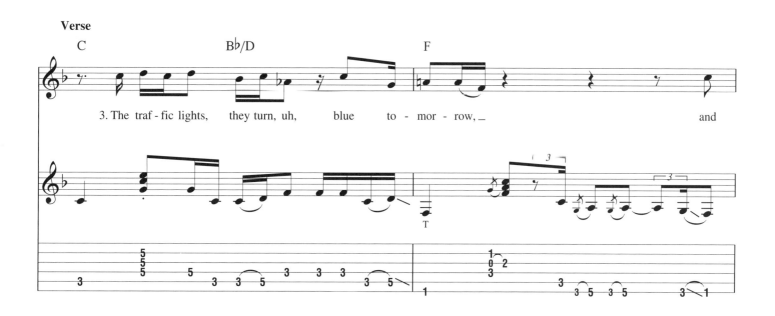

3. The traf-fic lights, they turn, uh, blue to - mor - row,__ and

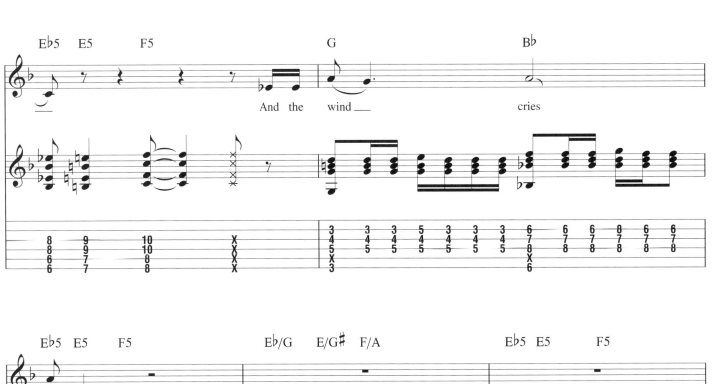

And the wind ___ cries

Mar - y.

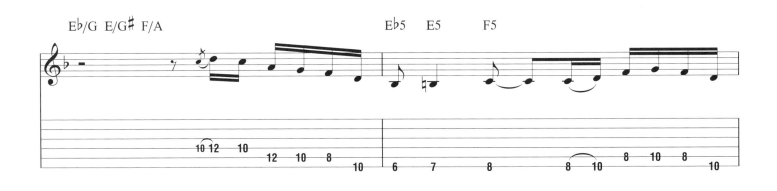

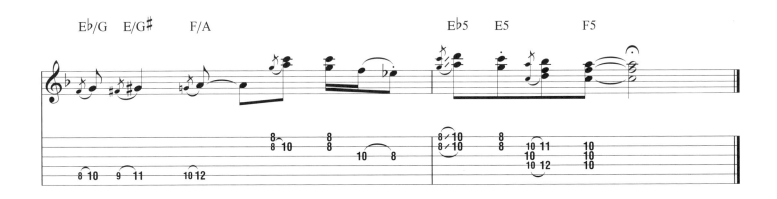

Can You See Me?

Words and Music by Jimi Hendrix

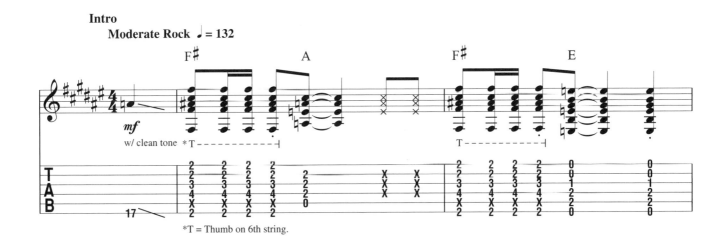

*T = Thumb on 6th string.

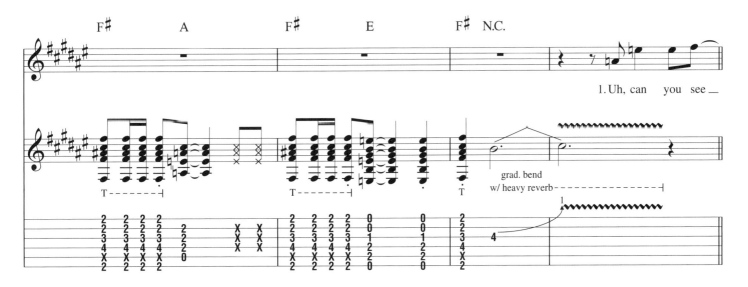

1. Uh, can you see

— me, — yeah,   beg - ging you — on my

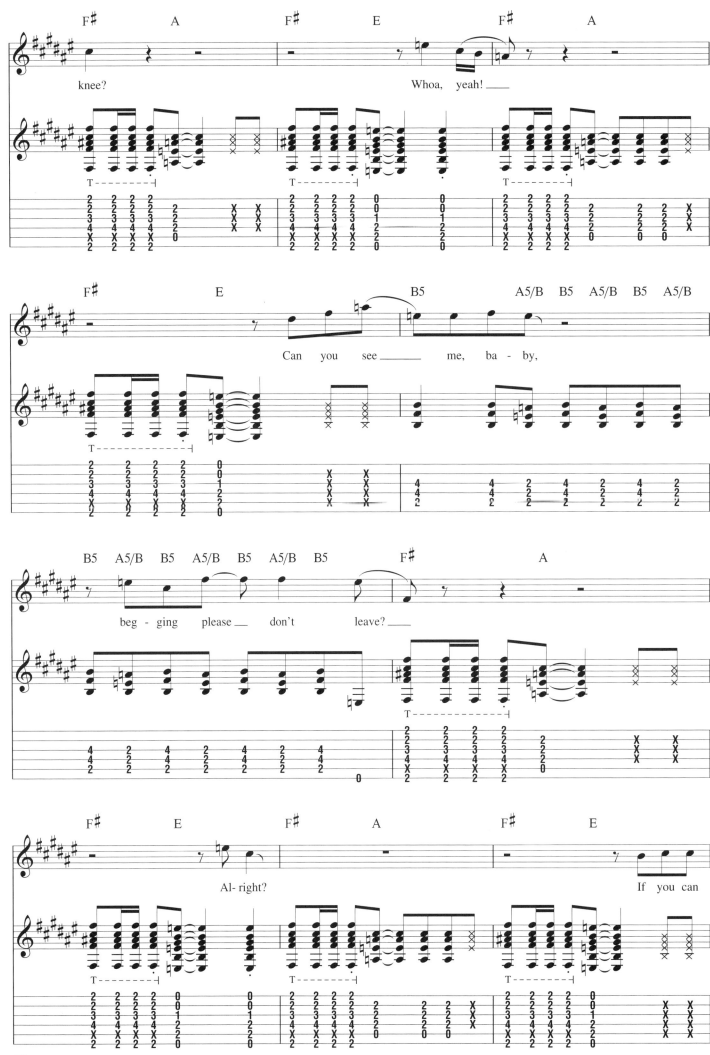

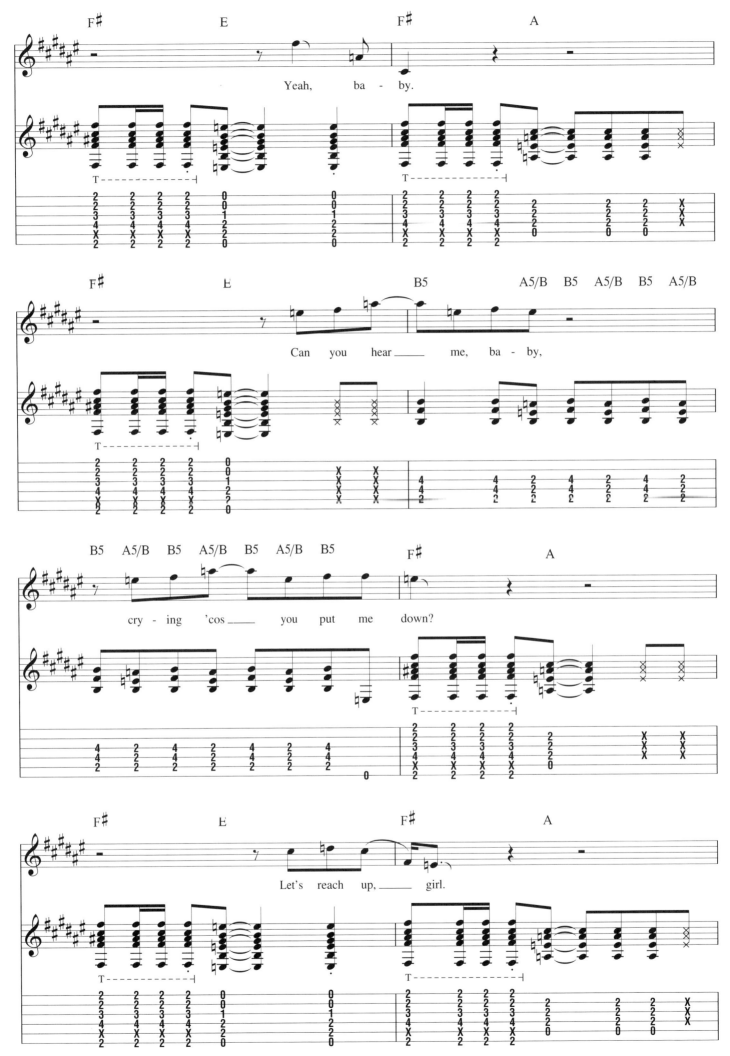

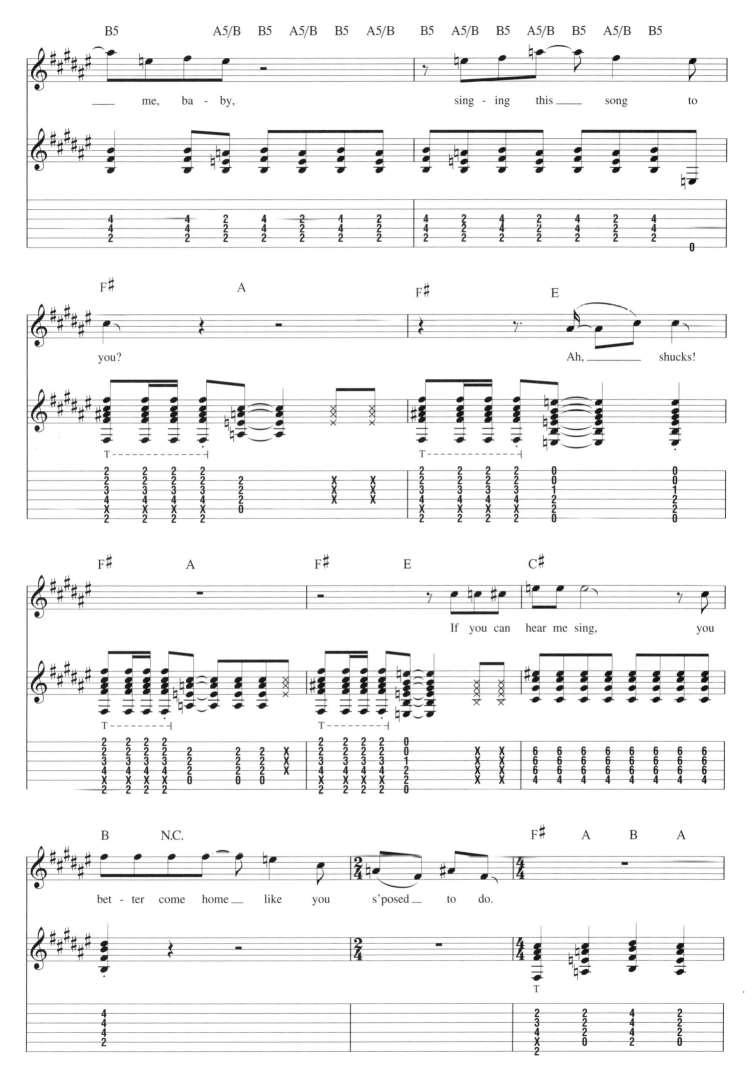

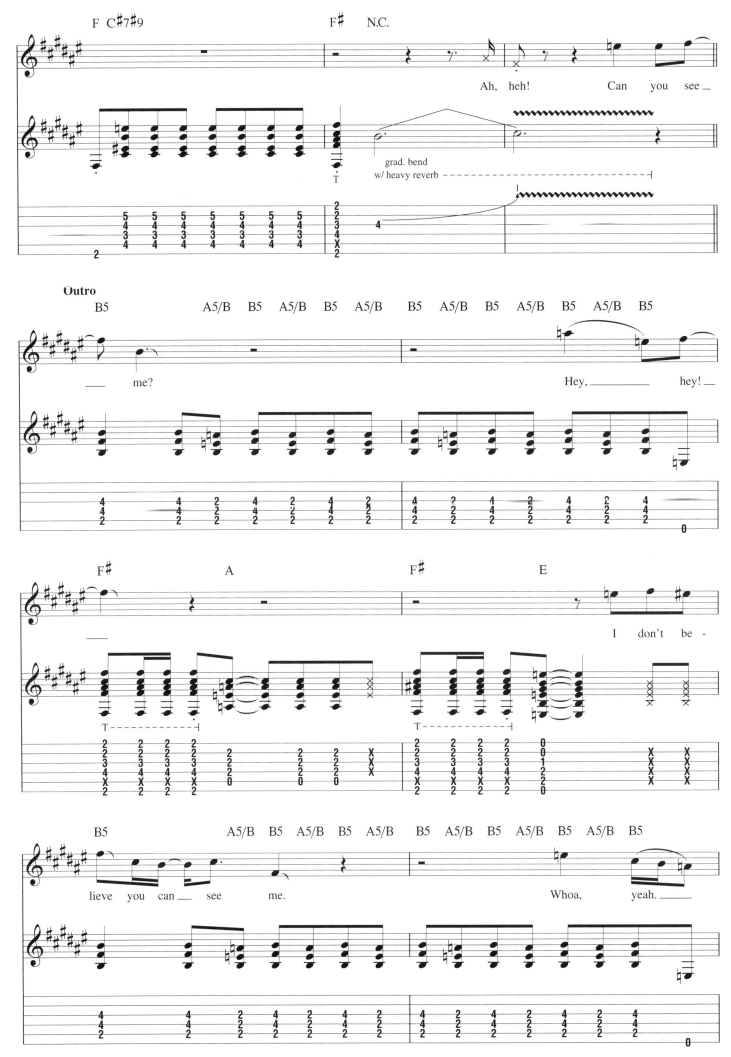

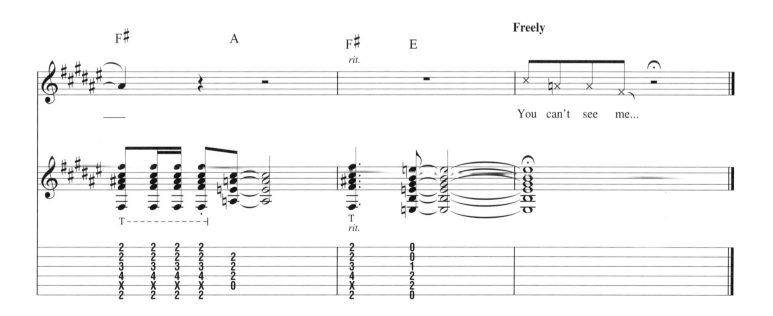

Hey Joe

Words and Music by Billy Roberts

Intro
Moderately slow Rock ♩ = 82

Verse

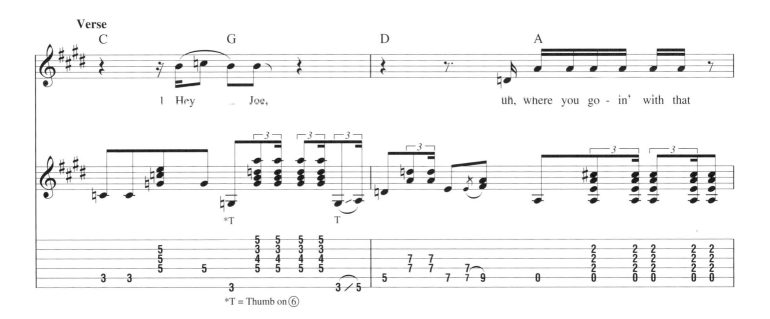

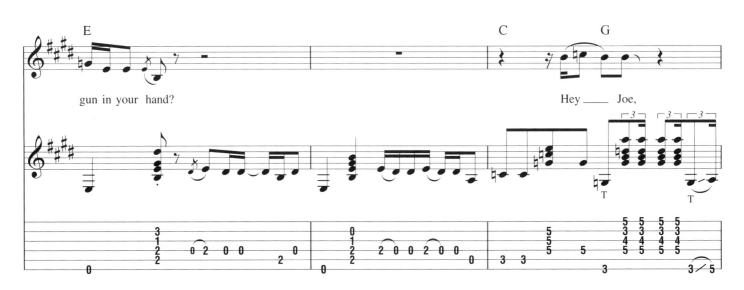

I heard you ___ shot ___ your old la-dy down, you shot her down in the ground. ___

Yeah! ___

Yes, I ___ did, I shot her,

you know I caught her mess-in' 'round, mess-in' 'round town. ___

Uh, yes I did, I shot her,

43

you know I ___ caught my old la - dy mess - in' 'round ___ town. ___ And I gave her the

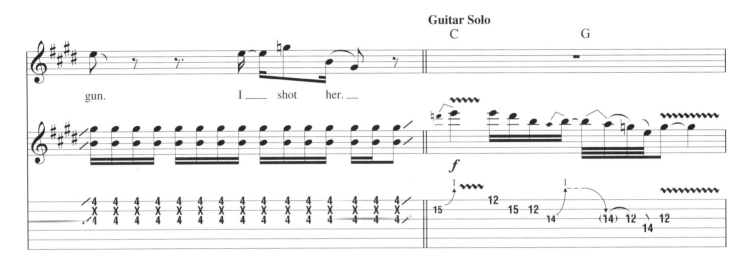

Guitar Solo

gun. I ___ shot her. ___

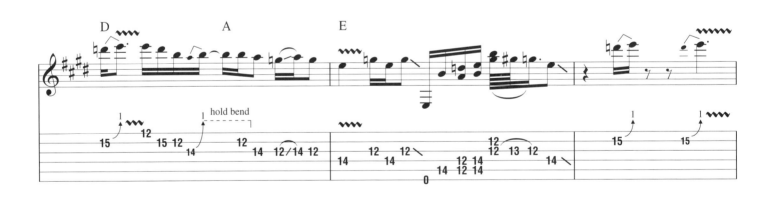

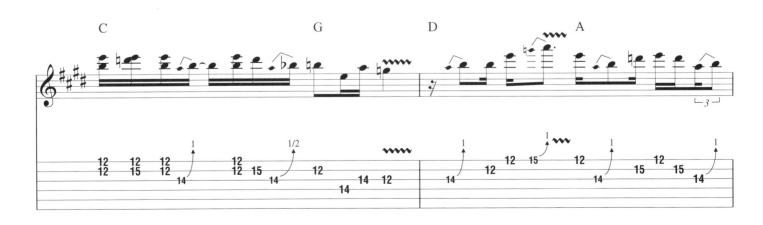

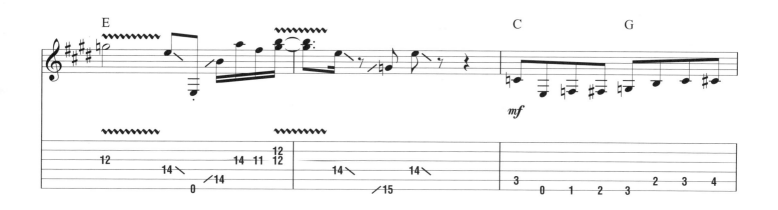

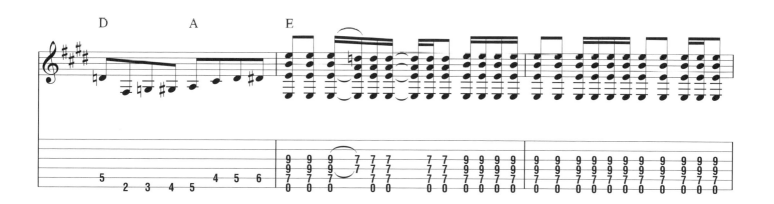

Verse

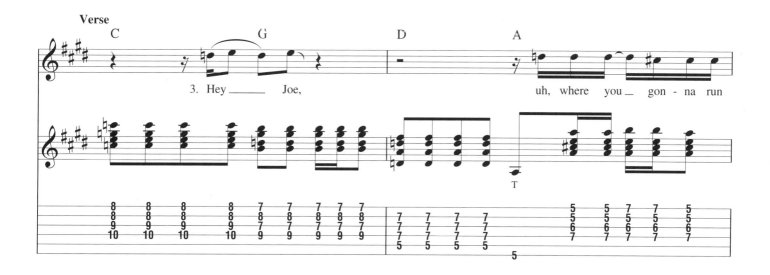

3. Hey _____ Joe,   uh, where you _ gon - na run

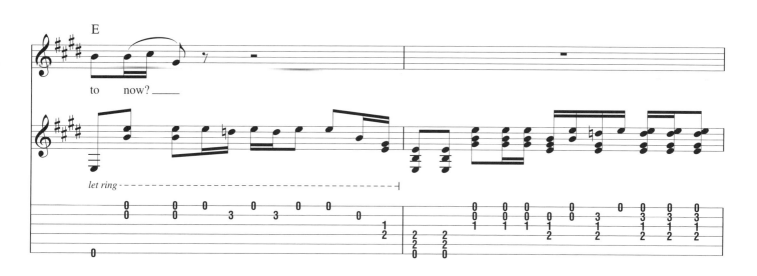

to   now? _____

All Along the Watchtower

Words and Music by Bob Dylan

Tune down 1/2 step:
(low to high) E♭-A♭-D♭-G♭-B♭-E♭

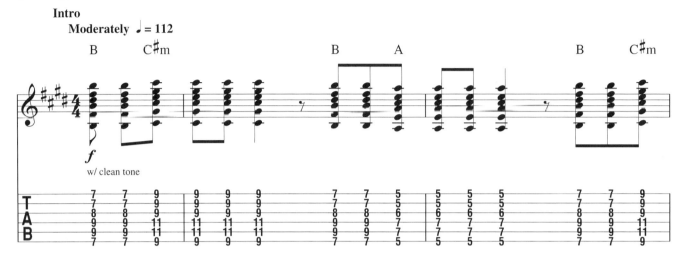

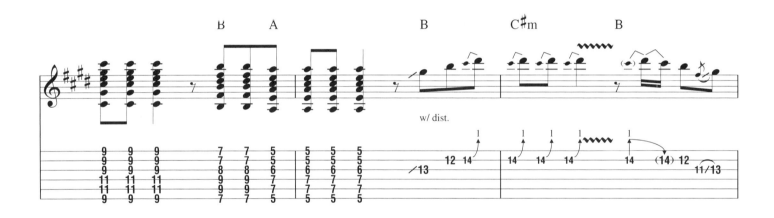

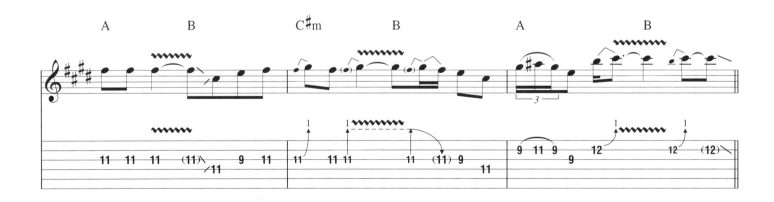

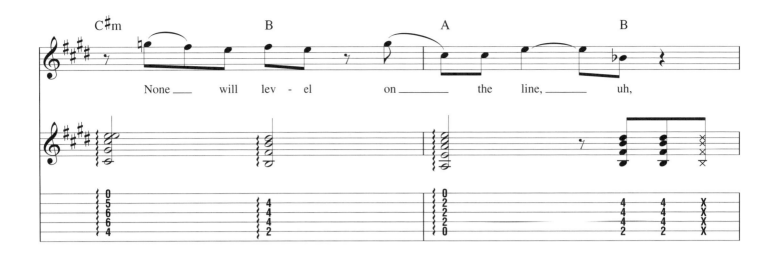

None ___ will lev - el on ___ the line, ___ uh,

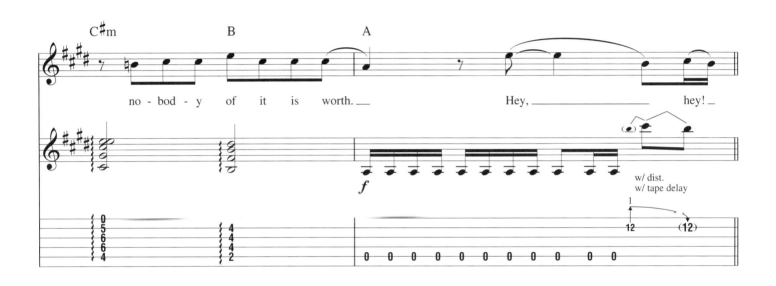

no - bod - y of it is worth. ___ Hey, ___ hey! ___

Guitar Solo

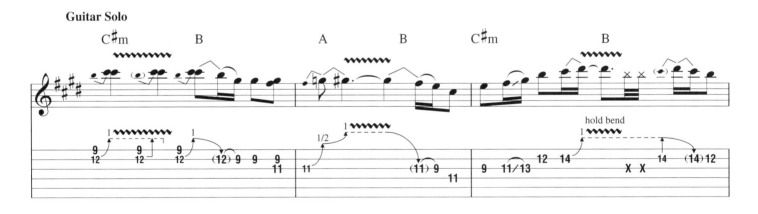

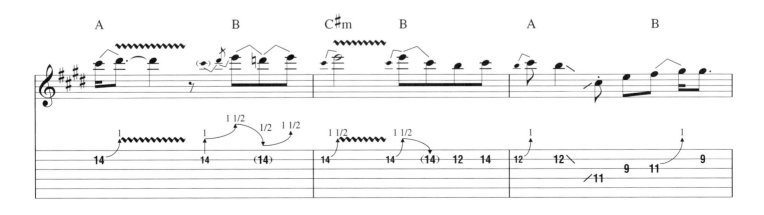

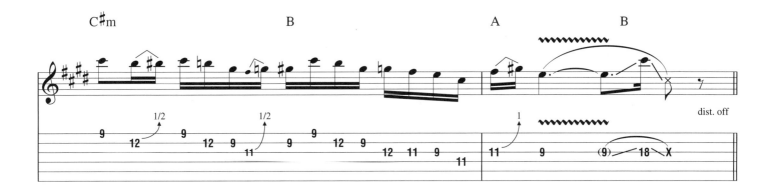

Verse

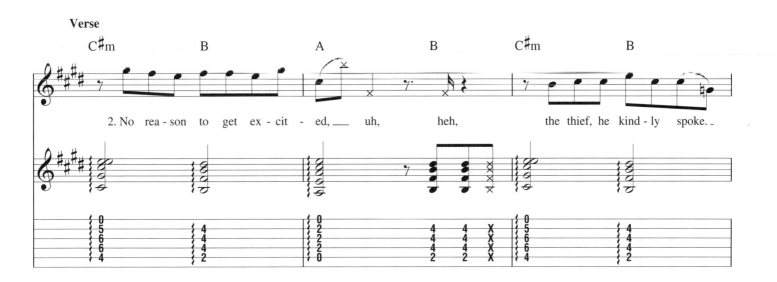

2. No rea-son to get ex-cit-ed, __ uh, heh, the thief, he kind-ly spoke. __

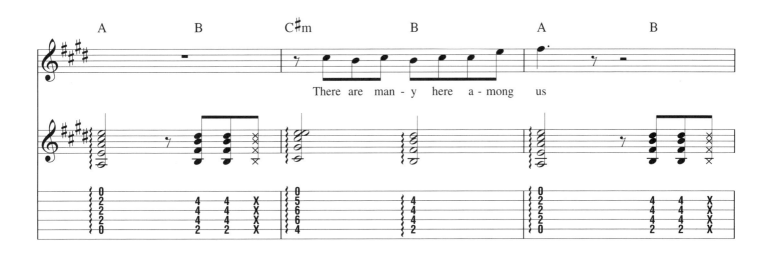

There are man-y here a-mong us

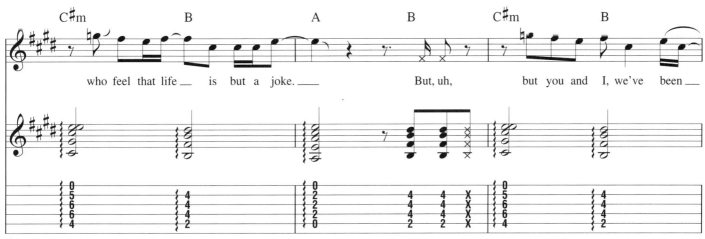

who feel that life __ is but a joke. __ But, uh, but you and I, we've been __

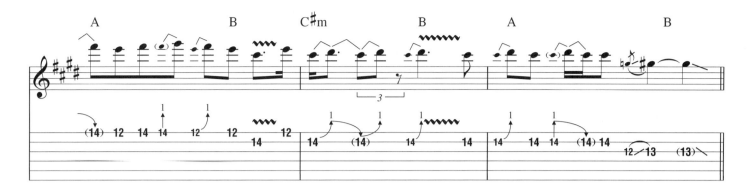

Interlude

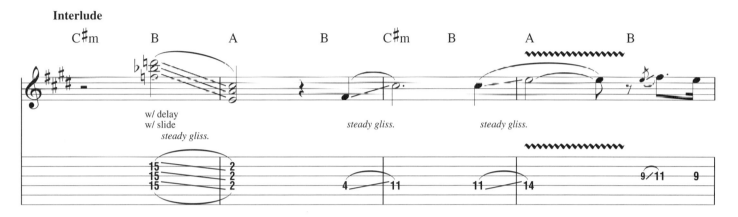

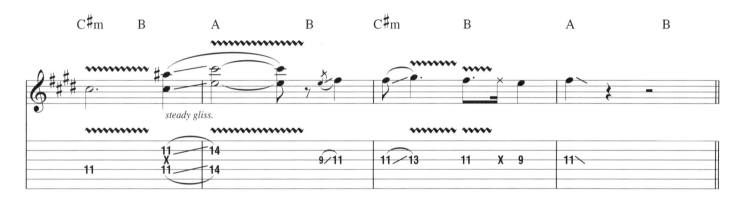

Guitar Solo

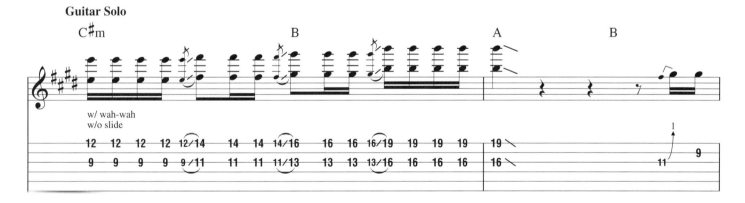

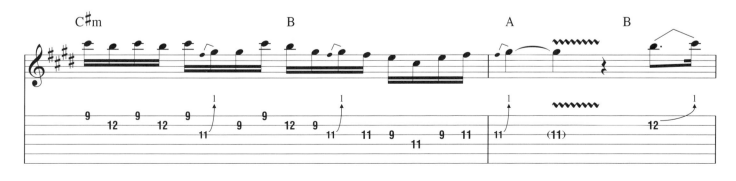

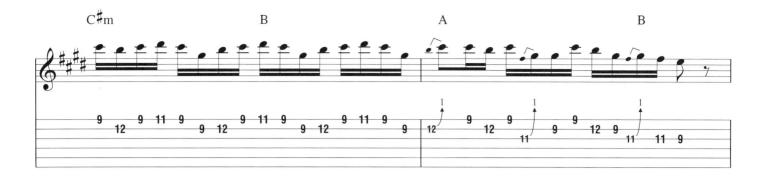

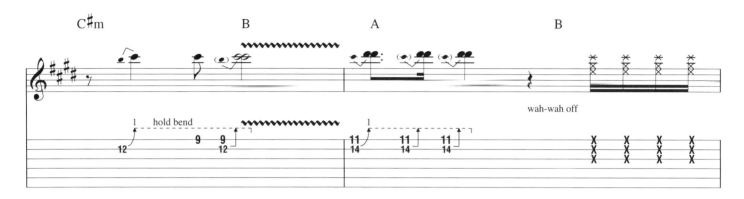

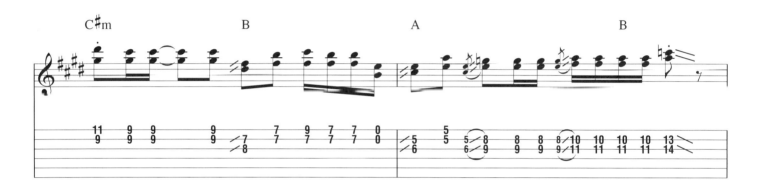

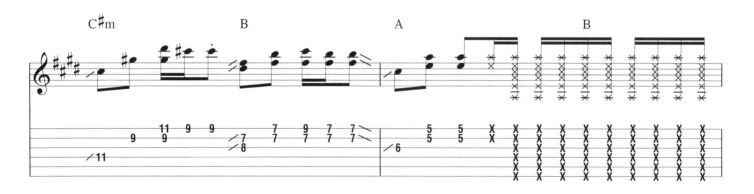

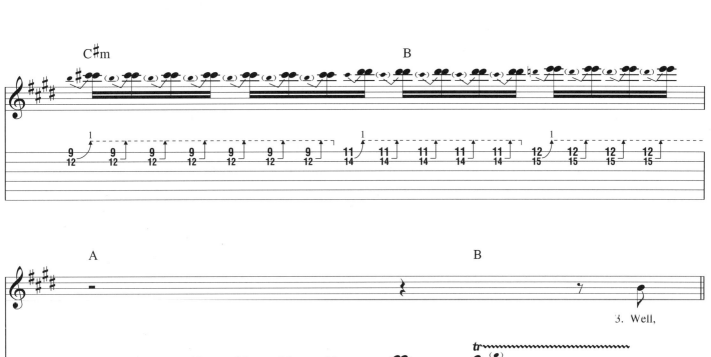

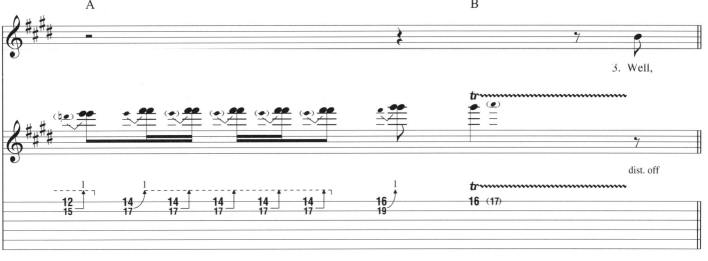

Verse

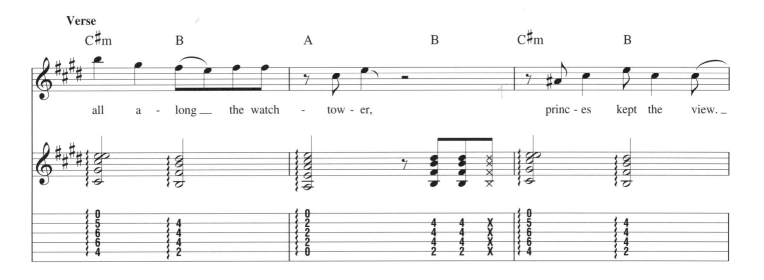

all a - long ___ the watch - tow - er,   princ - es kept the view. ___

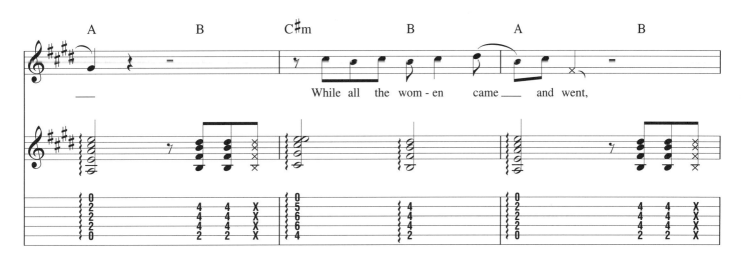

___   While all the wom - en came ___ and went,

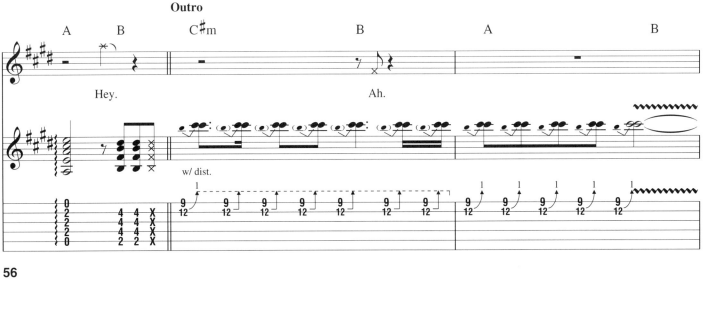

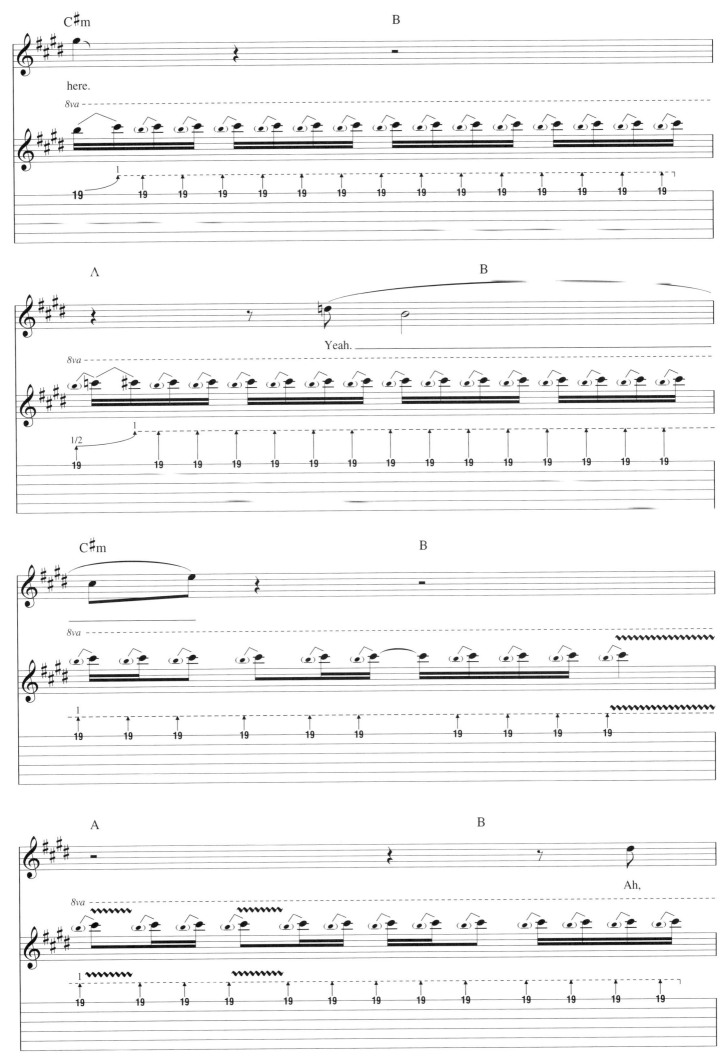

58

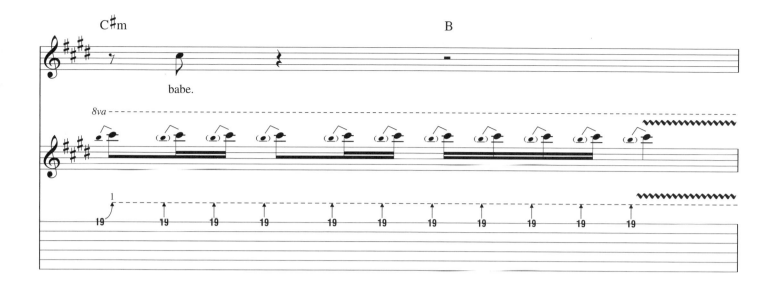

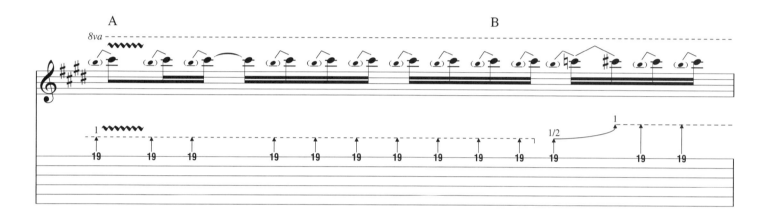

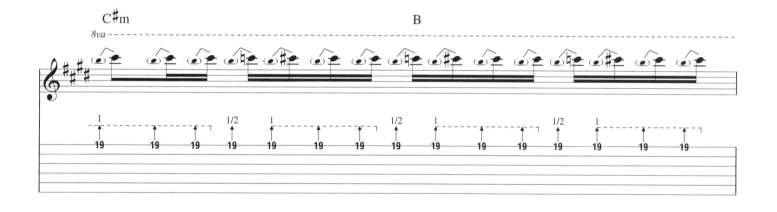

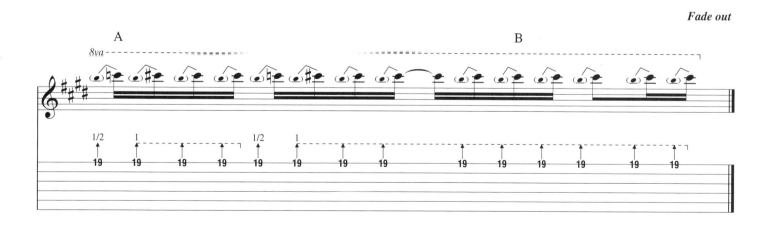

Stone Free

Words and Music by Jimi Hendrix

Intro
Moderate Rock ♩ = 132

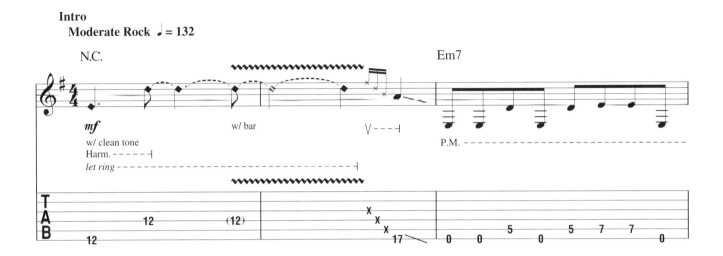

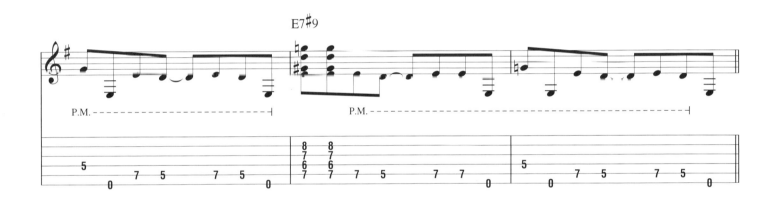

Verse
Em7

1. Ev - 'ry - day in the week I'm ___ in a dif - f'rent cit - y.

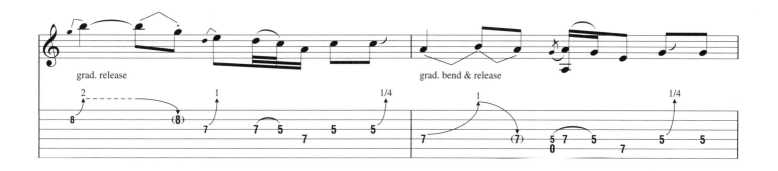

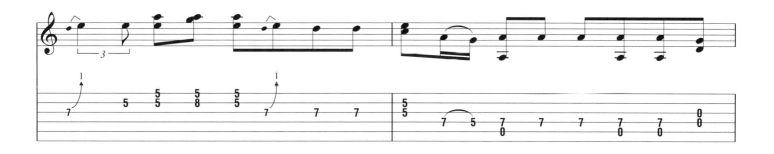

A7#9

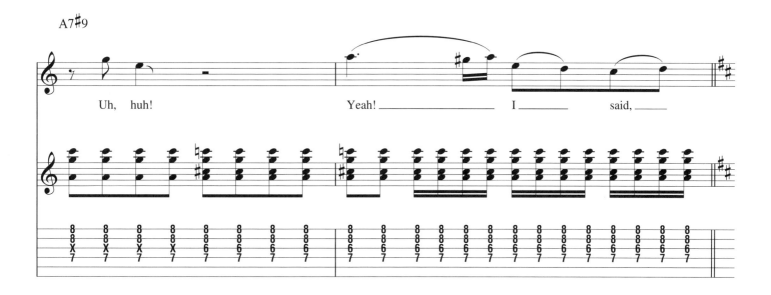

Uh, huh!   Yeah! _____ I _____ said,

Chorus

D

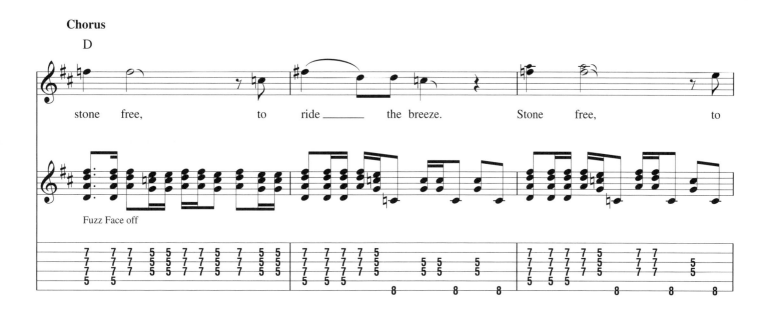

stone free,   to ride _____ the breeze.   Stone   free,   to

Fuzz Face off

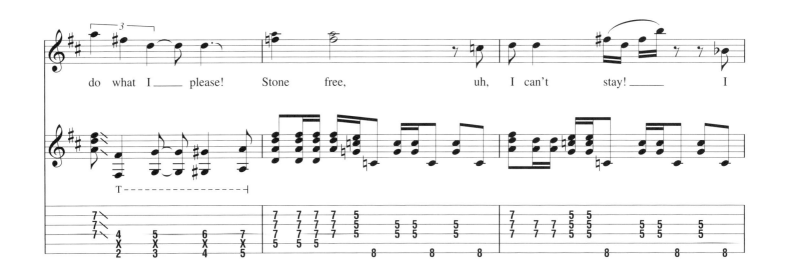

do what I ____ please! Stone free,   uh, I can't   stay! ____   I

(Stone   got to,   got to, got to get a - way!   Stone   free!   I'm

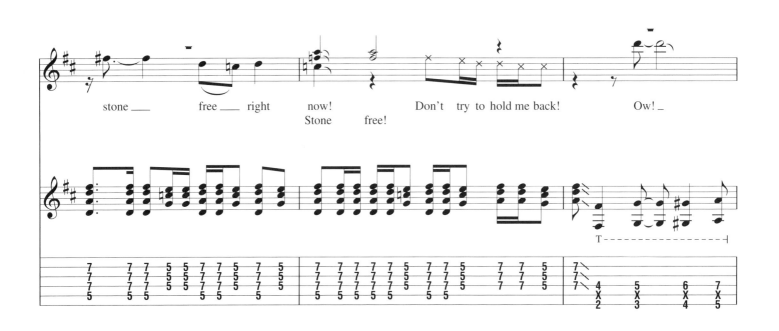

stone ____ free ____ right   now!   Don't try to hold me back!   Ow! _

Stone   free!

Outro

Faster ♩ = 160

Begin fade

Fade out

F5

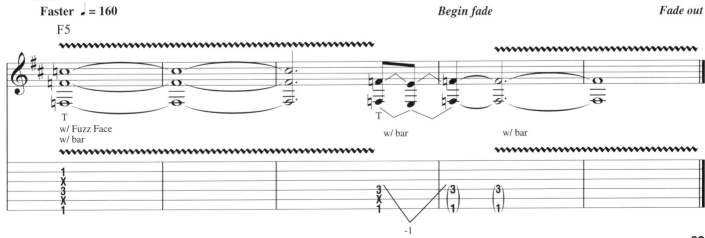

w/ Fuzz Face
w/ bar

w/ bar

w/ bar

-1

Crosstown Traffic

Words and Music by Jimi Hendrix

Tune down 1/2 step:
(low to high) E♭-A♭-D♭-G♭-B♭-E♭

Intro
Moderately ♩ = 116

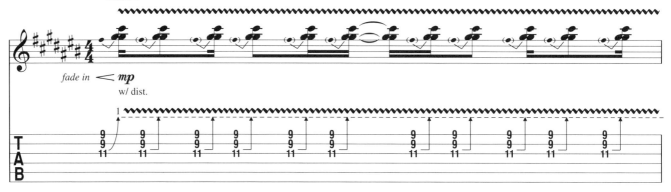

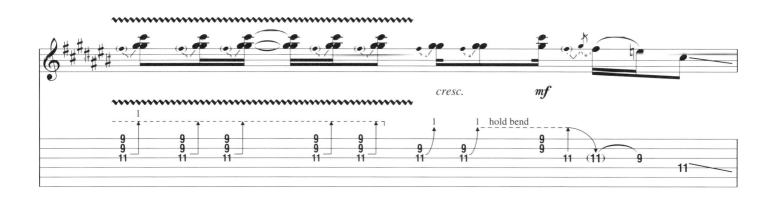

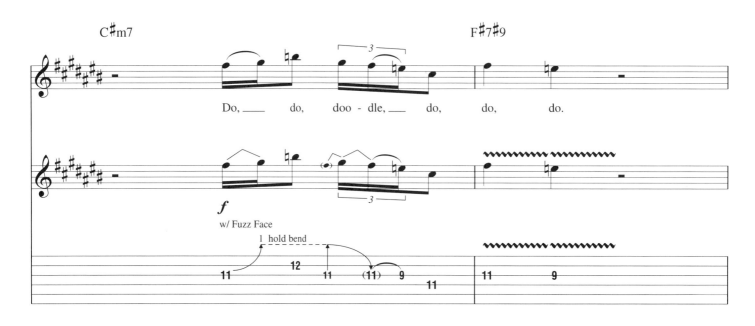

Do, ___ do, doo - dle, ___ do, do, do.

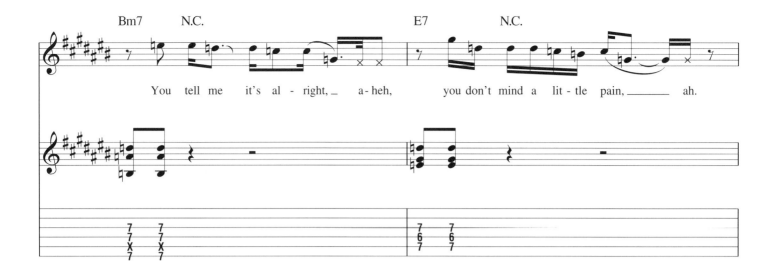

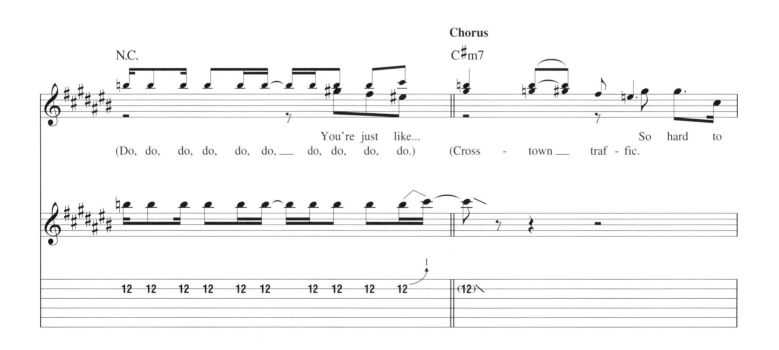

get through to you.
Do, do, doo - dle, __ do, do, do. Cross - town __ traf - fic.   I don't need to

run o - ver you.
Do, do, do, __ do, do, __ do,   do.
(Cross - town __ traf - fic.)   All you do is

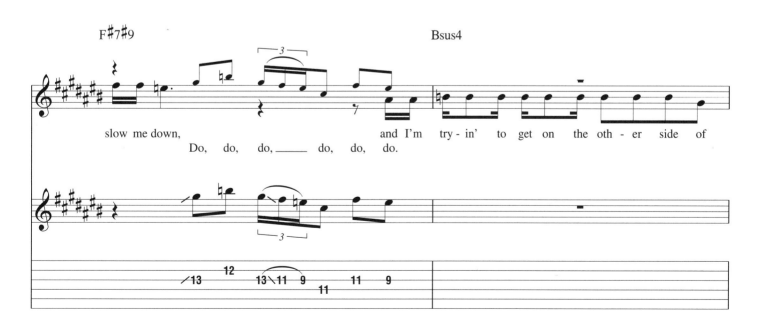

slow me down,   and I'm try - in' to get on the oth - er side of
Do, do, do, ____ do, do, do.

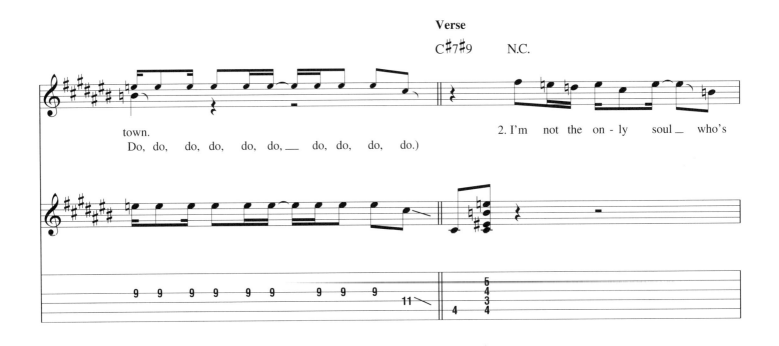

Verse

town.
Do, do,   do, do,   do, do,   do, do, do, do.)

2. I'm   not   the   on - ly   soul __   who's

ac - cused   of   hit   and   run. __

Tire __   tracks   all   a - cross   your   back;   I   can

hey,   I   can   see __   you   had __   your   fun. __   But,   ah,

dar - lin',   can't   you   see   my   sig -

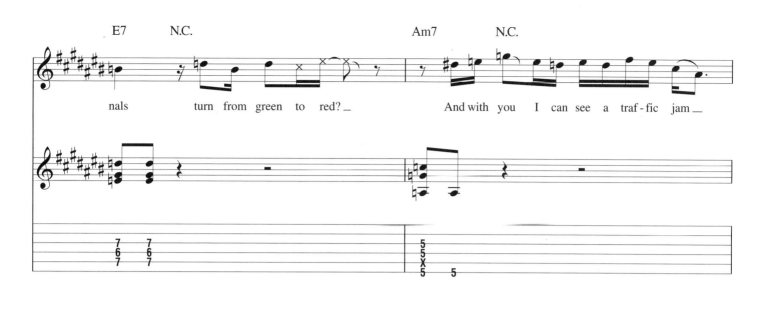

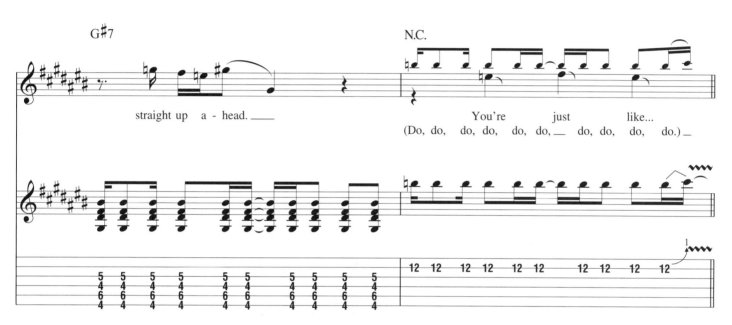

C#m7   F#7#9

I don't need to run o-ver you.

Cross - town ___ traf - fic.   Do, do, do, ___ do, do, ___ do.

C#m7   F#7#9

All ___ you do is slow me down, ___   an' I

Cross - town ___ traf - fic.   Do, do, doo - dle, ___ do, do, do.

Bsus4

got   bet - ter things ___ on the oth - er side of town.

Do, do.)

Guitar Solo

(Do, do, ____ do, do, do, do, do, do, do, ____ do.

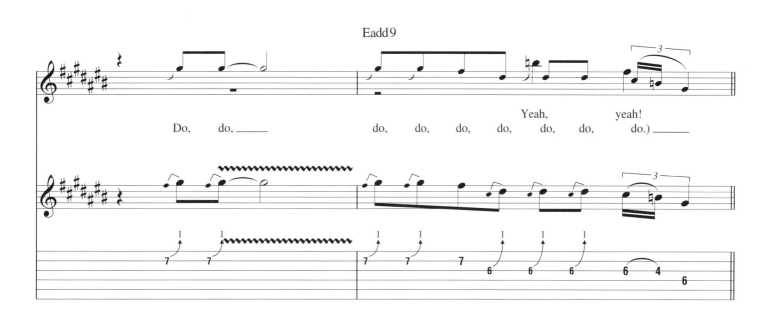

Do, do, ____ do, do, do, do, do, do, do.) ____

Yeah, yeah!

Chorus

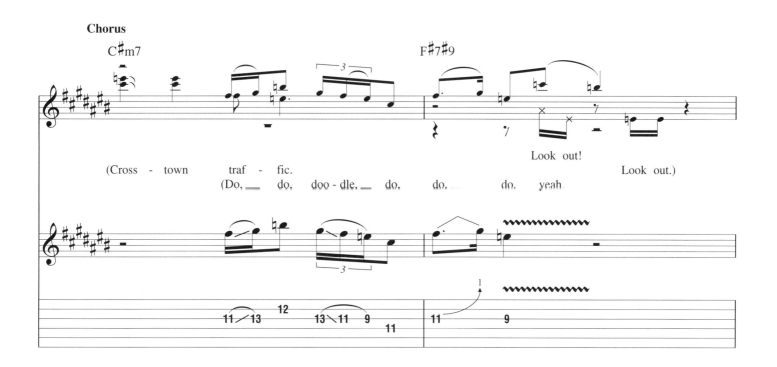

(Cross - town traf - fic.

(Do, ____ do, doo - dle, ____ do, do, do, yeah

Look out!

Look out.)

Look out, ba - by, com- in' through.
Do, do, do, do, do, do,— do, do, do, do, do, do, do, do,— do, do, do, do, do, do, do.

(Cross - town ___ traf - fic.)
Do, do, do, do, do, do, yeah.___ Look out.
Yeah!

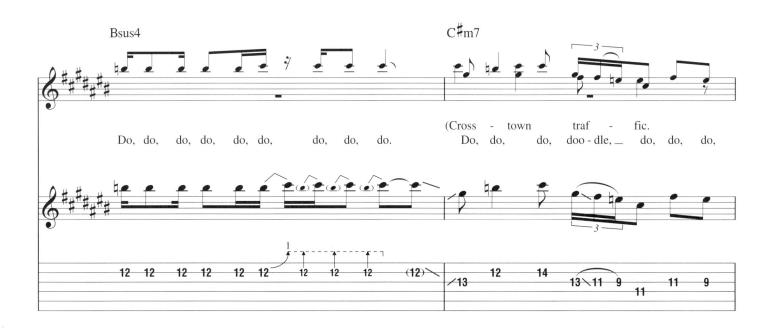

Do, do, do, do, do, do, do, do, do.
(Cross - town traf - fic.
Do, do, do, doo - dle,___ do, do, do,

Manic Depression

Words and Music by Jimi Hendrix

Tune down 1/2 step:
(low to high) E♭-A♭-D♭-G♭-B♭-E♭

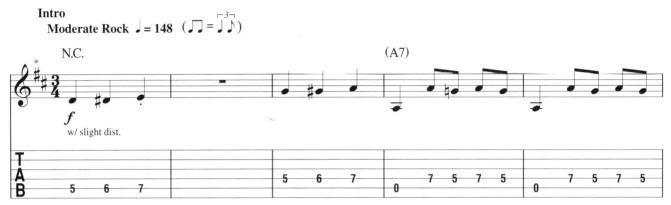

*Key signature denotes A Mixolydian.

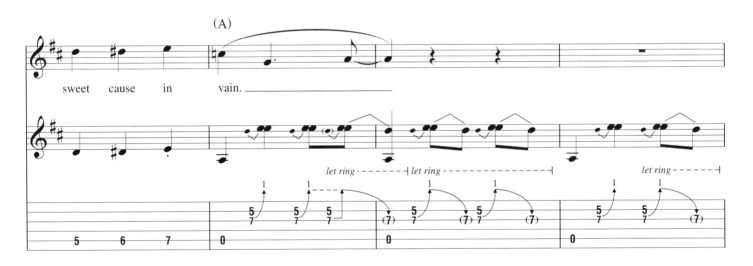

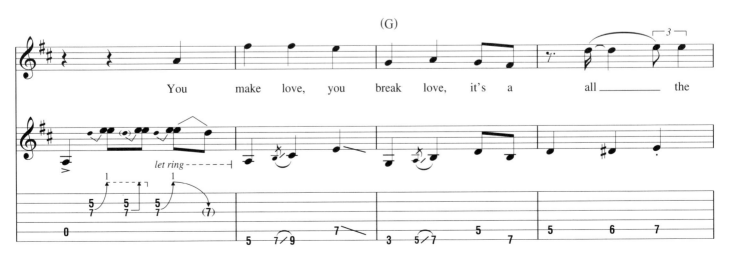

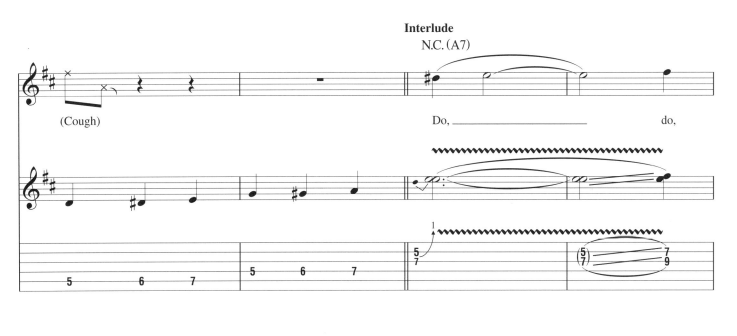

Interlude

N.C. (A7)

(Cough)

Do, _____ do,

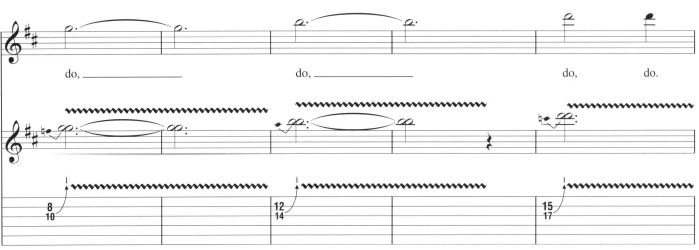

do, _____ do, _____ do, do.

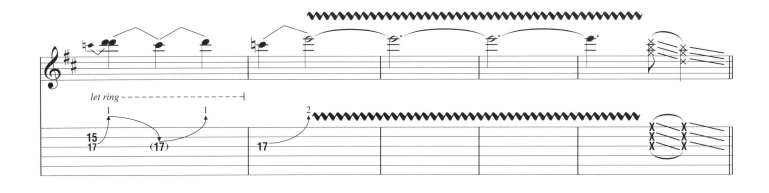

let ring - - - - - - - - - - - -

Guitar Solo

N.C. (A7)

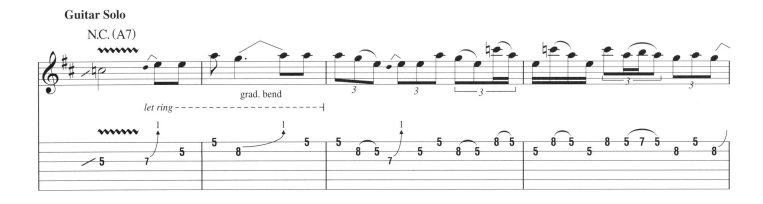

grad. bend

let ring - - - - - - - - - - - - - - - - -

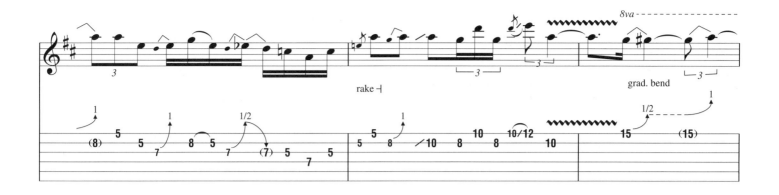

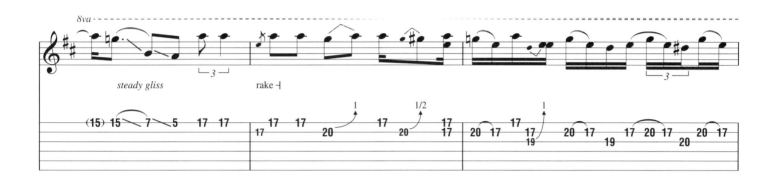

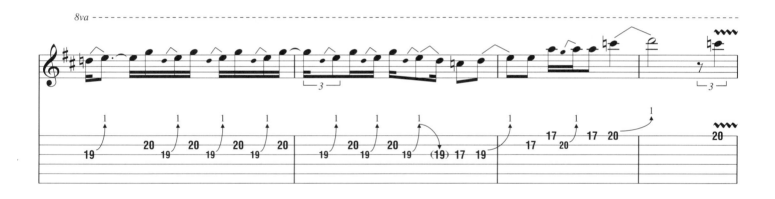

Cry— on— gui tar.

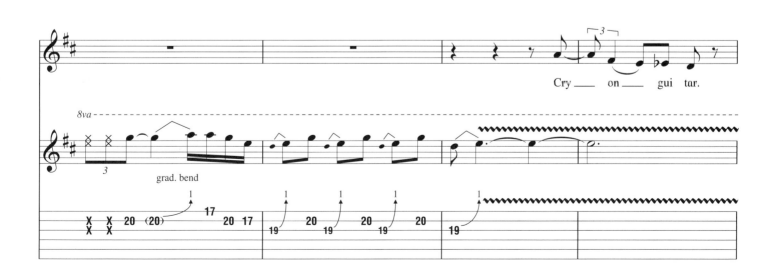

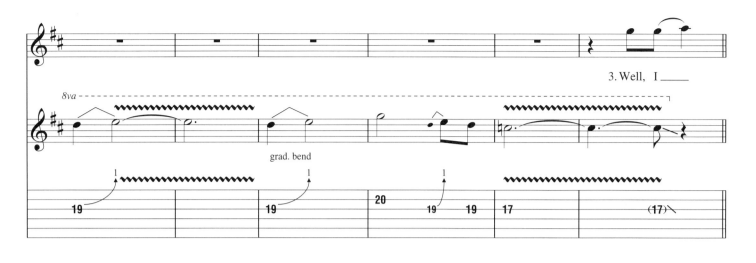

3. Well, I ____

Verse

think I'll go turn my-self off ____ and, uh, uh, huh, go on ____ down. ____

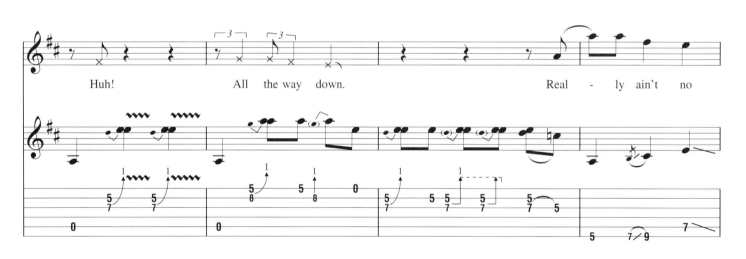

Huh! All the way down. Real - ly ain't no

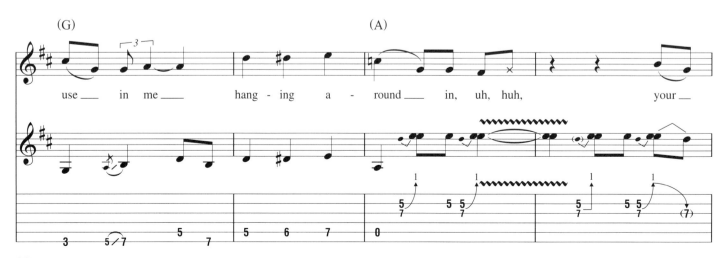

use ____ in me ____ hang-ing a - round ____ in, uh, huh, your ____

Outro

Mu - sic, sweet mu - sic, sweet mu - sic, sweet mu - sic, ah!

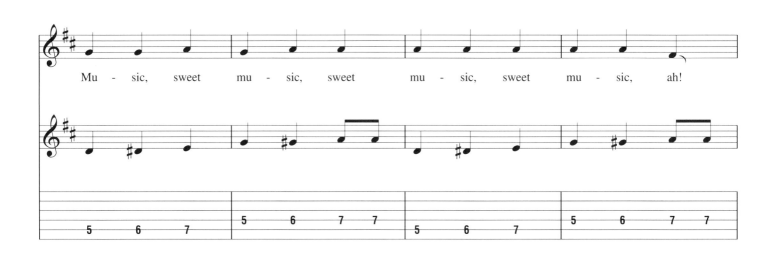

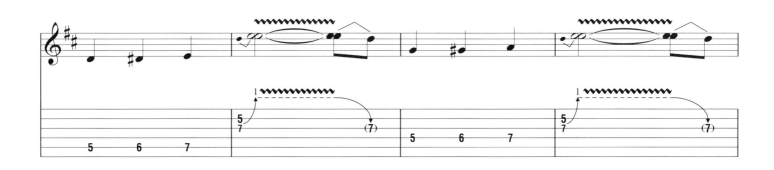

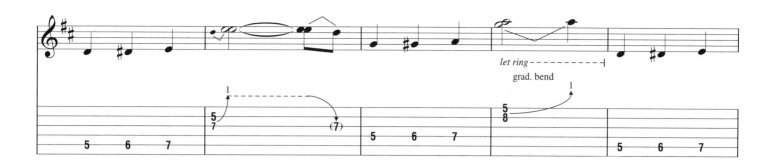

Mu - sic, sweet mu - sic, sweet mu - sic. Yeah!

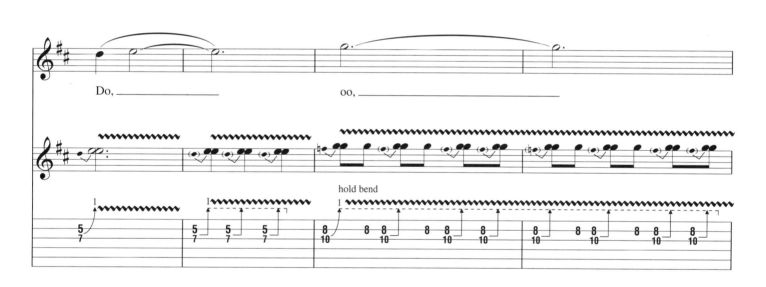

Do,_____ oo,_____

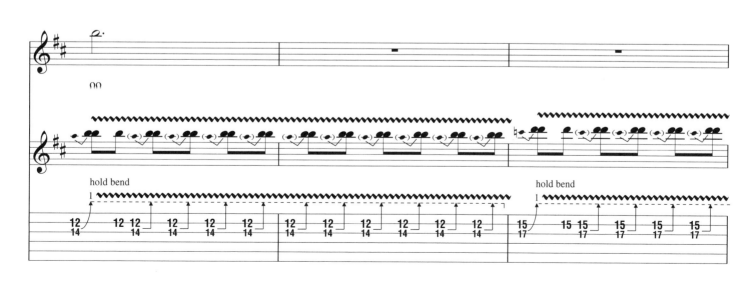

oo

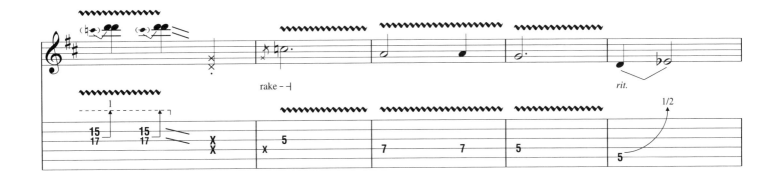

rake

rit.

Free time

A5

Hmm, hmm, hmm. De - press...

fdbk.

Fade out

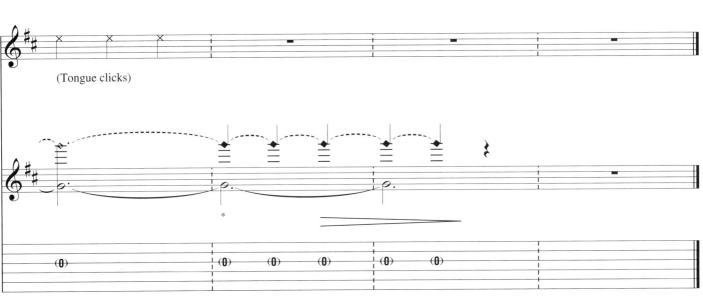

(Tongue clicks)

*Switch pickup selector between neck & middle pickups, sounding fdbk. at specified rhythm.

Remember

Words and Music by Jimi Hendrix

Tune down 1/2 step:
(low to high) E♭-A♭-D♭-G♭-B♭-E♭

Intro

Moderately slow Rock ♩ = 98

1. Oh, ___ re-

Verse

mem - ber the mock - ing - bird, my ba - by bun. He used to

*T = Thumb on 6th string.

sing for his sup - per, ba - by. Yes, ___ he used to sing ___

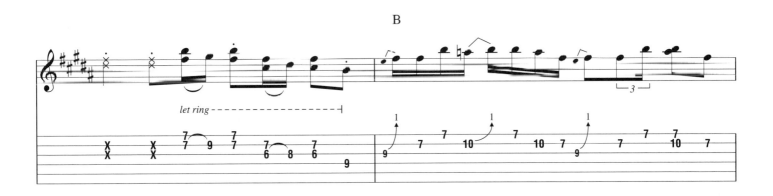

Verse

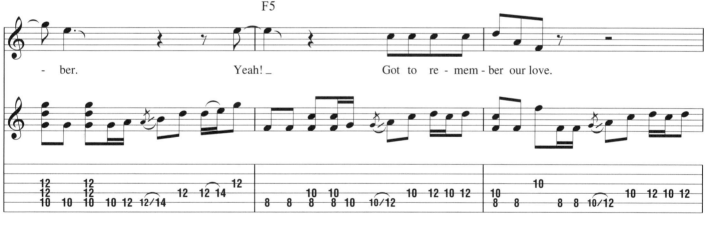

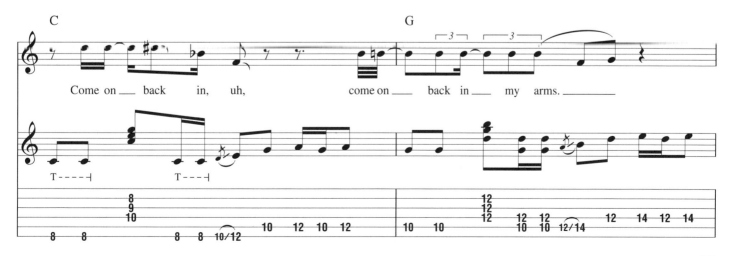

Make ev - 'ry - thing __ that __ bet - ter.

Outro

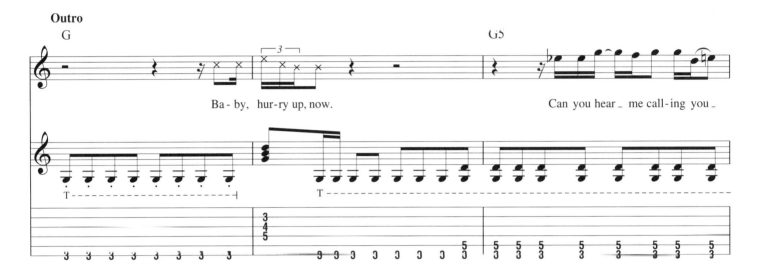

Ba - by, hur-ry up, now.   Can you hear __ me call-ing you __

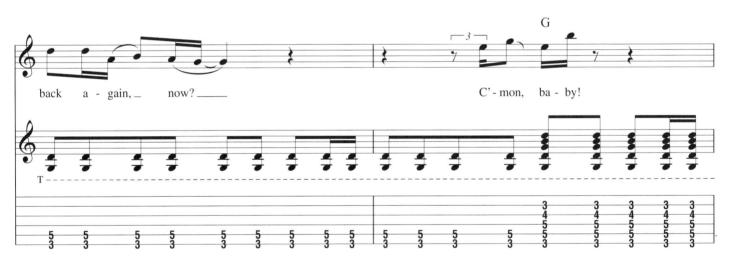

back   a - gain, __   now? _____   C' - mon,   ba - by!

Begin fade   *Fade out*

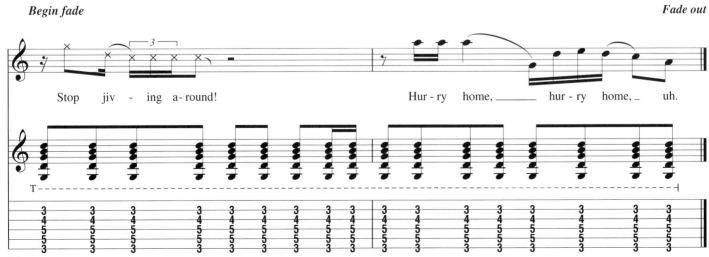

Stop   jiv - ing a - round!   Hur - ry   home, _____   hur - ry   home, _ uh.

Red House

Words and Music by Jimi Hendrix

Tune down 1/2 step:
(low to high) Eb-Ab-Db-Gb-Bb-Eb

Intro

Moderately slow Blues ♩. = 66

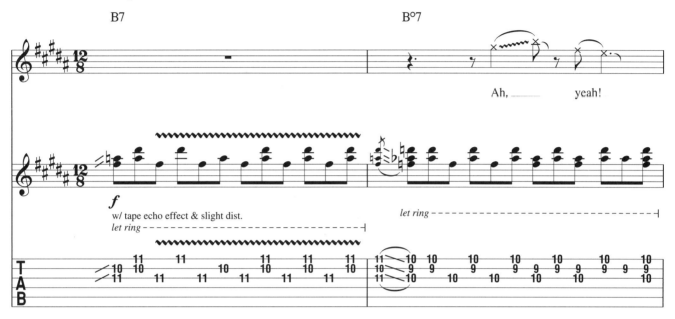

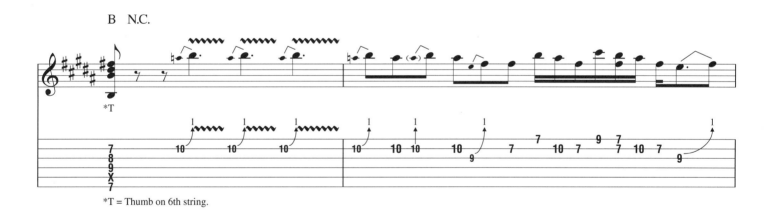

*T = Thumb on 6th string.

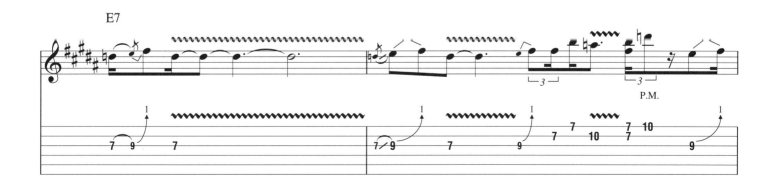

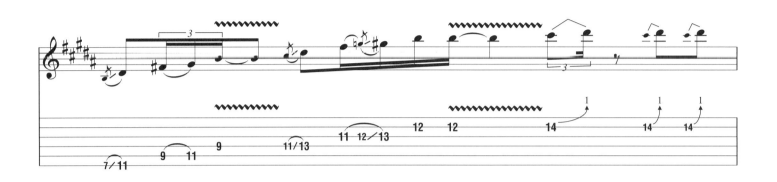

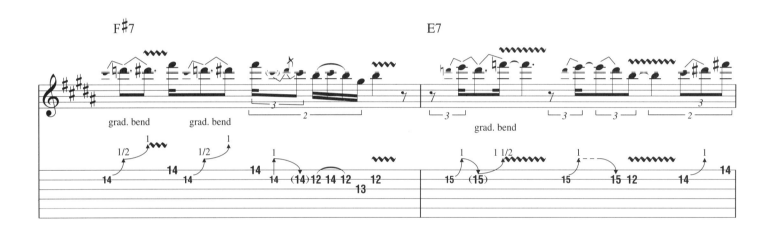

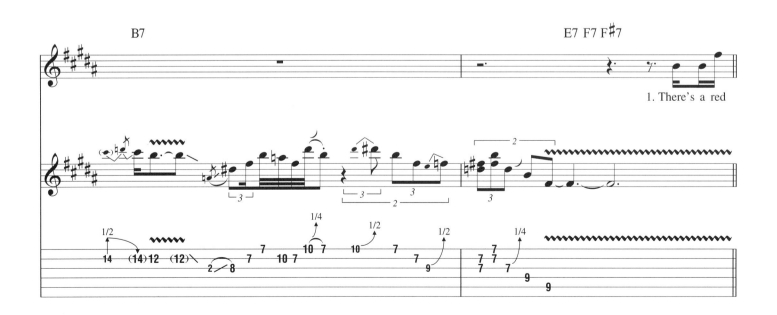

I ain't been home to see my — ba - by —   in nine - ty - nine and one - half days. —

2. Wait a

Verse

min - ute, some - thing's wrong here, —   the key won't un - lock the door. —

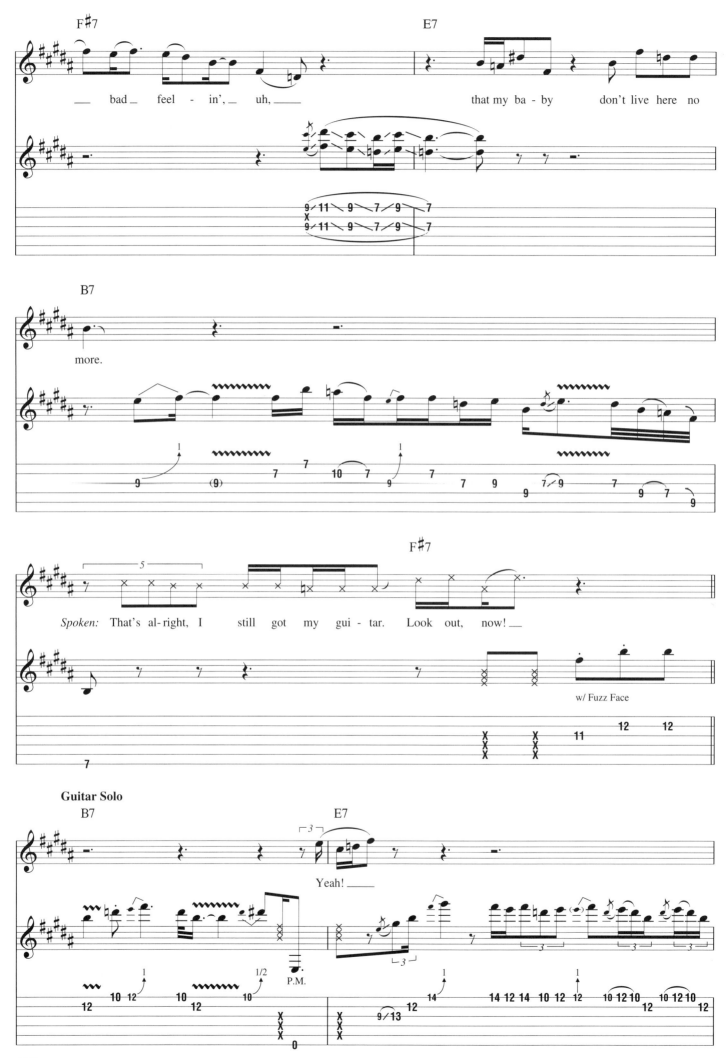

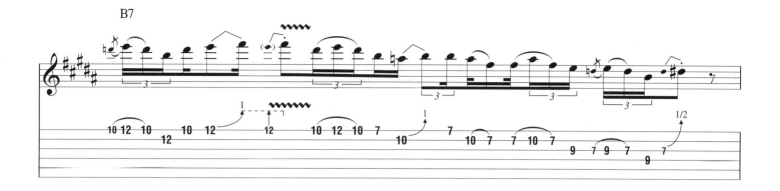

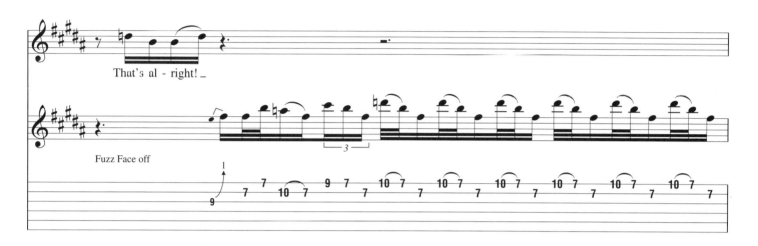

That's al - right! _

Fuzz Face off

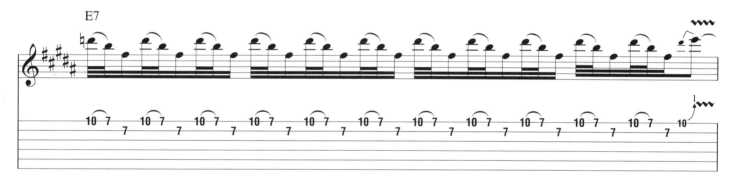

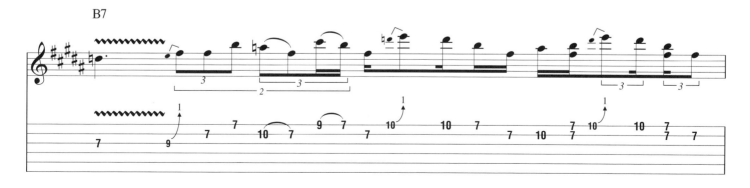

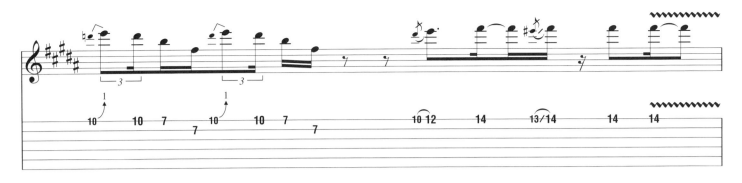

F#7

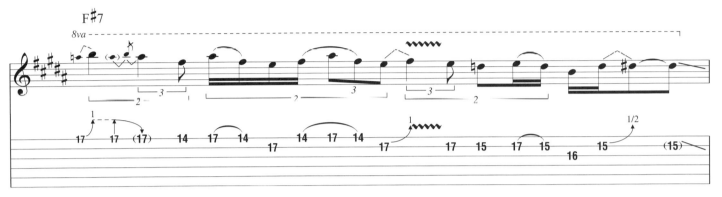

E7

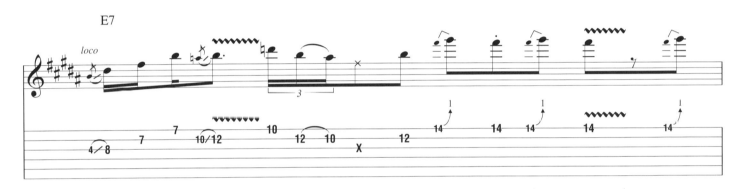

B7

F#7

3. Well, I might as well, uh, ___

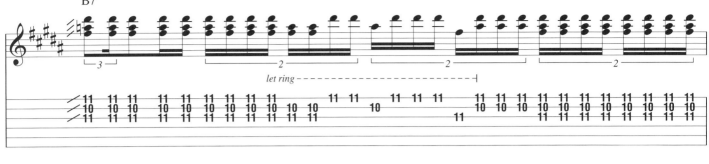

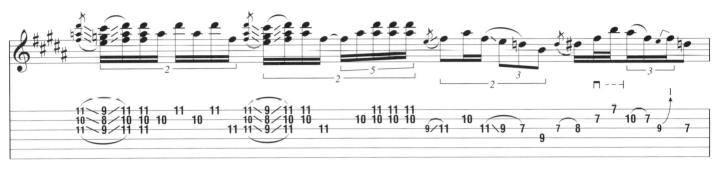

'Cos if my ba-by don't love me no more,

I know her sis-ter will!

Free time

Yeah!

w/ Fuzz Face

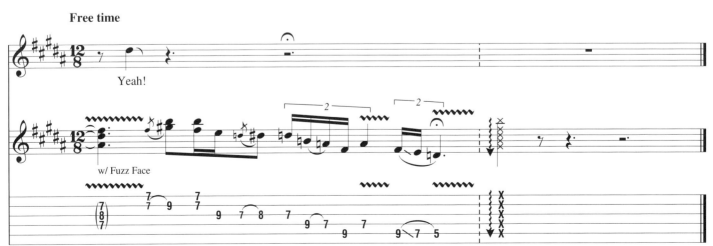

Foxey Lady

Words and Music by Jimi Hendrix

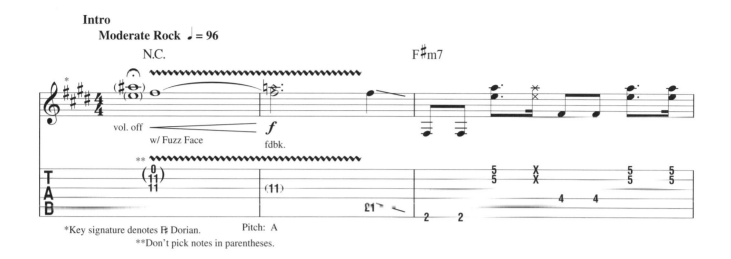

*Key signature denotes F# Dorian. Pitch: A
**Don't pick notes in parentheses.

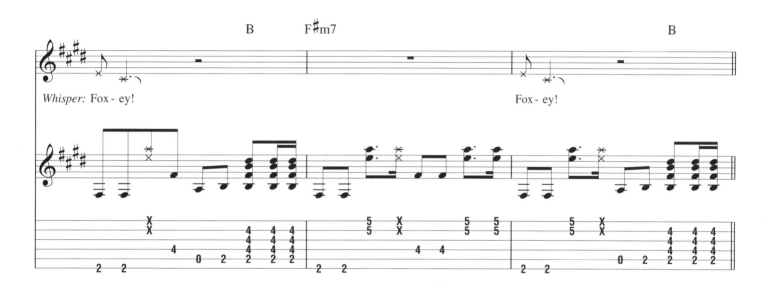

no. ___ You've got to be all mine, all ___ mine.

Free time
N.C.

A tempo

Fox-ey la - dy! ___ Here I come, ba - by. I'm com-in' to get ya!

vol. off

*

*Don't pick notes in parentheses.

Outro

Ow! Fox-ey la - dy, ___ yeah, yeah, ___ ooh! You look so good! ___
Fox - ey!

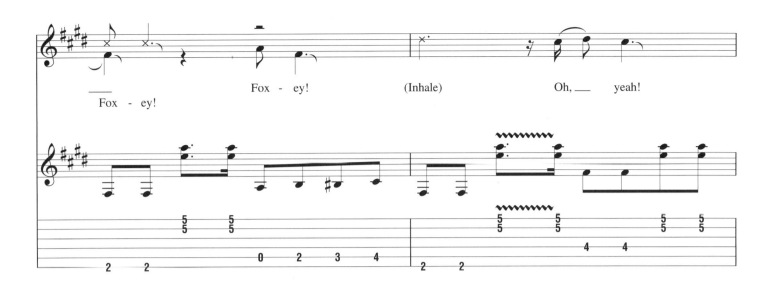

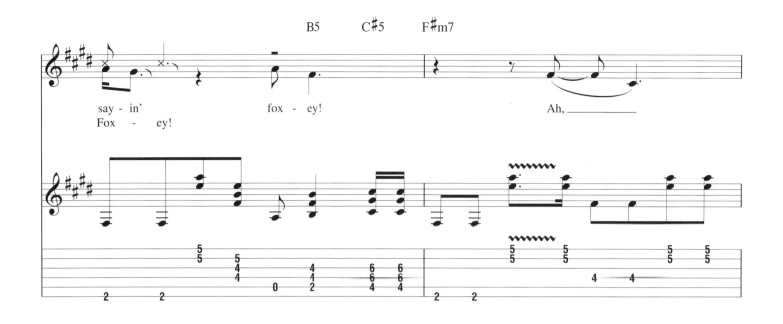

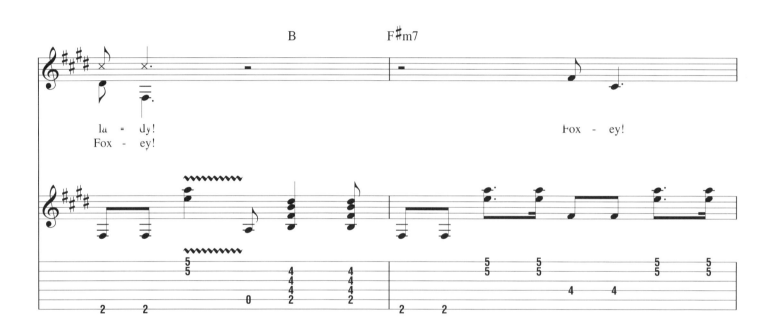

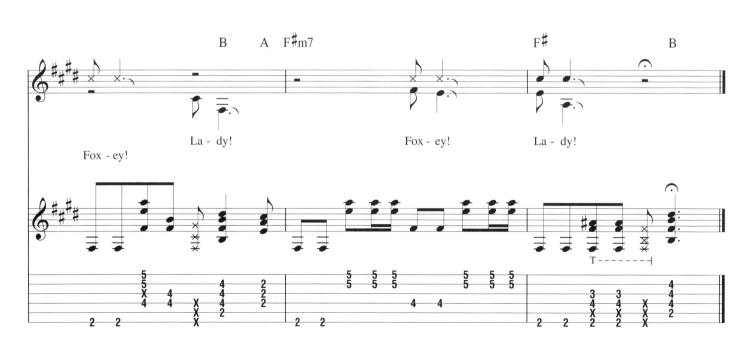

Guitar Notation Legend

Notes:

THE MUSICAL STAFF shows pitches and rhythms and is divided by bar lines into measures. Pitches are named after the first seven letters of the alphabet.

TABLATURE graphically represents the guitar fingerboard. Each horizontal line represents a string, and each number represents a fret.

Strings:

4th string, 2nd fret   1st & 2nd strings open, played together   open D chord

HALF-STEP BEND: Strike the note and bend up 1/2 step.

WHOLE-STEP BEND: Strike the note and bend up one step.

GRACE NOTE BEND: Strike the note and bend up as indicated. The first note does not take up any time.

SLIGHT (MICROTONE) BEND: Strike the note and bend up 1/4 step.

BEND AND RELEASE: Strike the note and bend up as indicated, then release back to the original note. Only the first note is struck.

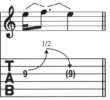

PRE-BEND: Bend the note as indicated, then strike it.

VIBRATO: The string is vibrated by rapidly bending and releasing the note with the fretting hand.

PALM MUTING: The note is partially muted by the pick hand lightly touching the string(s) just before the bridge.

HAMMER-ON: Strike the first (lower) note with one finger, then sound the higher note (on the same string) with another finger by fretting it without picking.

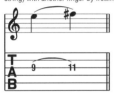

PULL-OFF: Place both fingers on the notes to be sounded. Strike the first note and without picking, pull the finger off to sound the second (lower) note.

LEGATO SLIDE: Strike the first note and then slide the same fret-hand finger up or down to the second note. The second note is not struck.

SHIFT SLIDE: Same as legato slide, except the second note is struck.

TRILL: Very rapidly alternate between the notes indicated by continuously hammering on and pulling off.

TAPPING: Hammer ("tap") the fret indicated with the pick-hand index or middle finger and pull off to the note fretted by the fret hand.

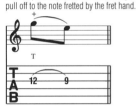

NATURAL HARMONIC: Strike the note while the fret-hand lightly touches the string directly over the fret indicated.

PINCH HARMONIC: The note is fretted normally and a harmonic is produced by adding the edge of the thumb or the tip of the index finger of the pick hand to the normal pick attack.

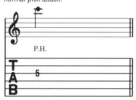

TREMOLO PICKING: The note is picked as rapidly and continuously as possible.

VIBRATO BAR DIVE AND RETURN: The pitch of the note or chord is dropped a specified number of steps (in rhythm) then returned to the original pitch.

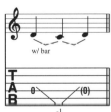

VIBRATO BAR SCOOP: Depress the bar just before striking the note, then quickly release the bar.

VIBRATO BAR DIP: Strike the note and then immediately drop a specified number of steps, then release back to the original pitch.

Additional Musical Definitions

(accent) • Accentuate note (play it louder)

(staccato) • Play the note short

D.S. al Coda • Go back to the sign (𝄋), then play until the measure marked *"To Coda,"* then skip to the section labelled *"Coda."*

D.C. al Fine • Go back to the beginning of the song and play until the measure marked *"Fine"* (end).

Fill • Label used to identify a brief melodic figure which is to be inserted into the arrangement.

N.C. • Instrument is silent (drops out).

• Repeat measures between signs.

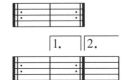

• When a repeated section has different endings, play the first ending only the first time and the second ending only the second time.

Guitar Recorded Versions®

AUTHENTIC TRANSCRIPTIONS WITH NOTES AND TABLATURE

Guitar Recorded Versions® are note-for-note transcriptions of guitar music taken directly off recordings. This series, one of the most popular in print today, features some of the greatest guitar players and groups from blues and rock to country and jazz. Guitar Recorded Versions are transcribed by the best transcribers in the business. Every book contains notes and tablature.

GUITAR RECORDED VERSIONS

AUTHENTIC TRANSCRIPTIONS WITH NOTES AND TABLATURE

HAL•LEONARD GUITAR PLAY•ALONG

This series will help you play your favorite songs quickly and easily. Just follow the tab and listen to the CD to hear how the guitar should sound, and then play along using the separate backing tracks. Mac or PC users can also slow down the tempo by using the CD in their computer. The melody and lyrics are included in the book so that you can sing or simply follow along.

INCLUDES TAB

VOL. 1 – ROCK GUITAR   00699570 / $12.95
Day Tripper • Message in a Bottle • Refugee • Shattered • Sunshine of Your Love • Takin' Care of Business • Tush • Walk This Way.

VOL. 2 – ACOUSTIC   00699569 / $12.95
Angie • Behind Blue Eyes • Best of My Love • Blackbird • Dust in the Wind • Layla • Night Moves • Yesterday.

VOL. 3 – HARD ROCK   00699573 / $14.95
Crazy Train • Iron Man • Living After Midnight • Rock You Like a Hurricane • Round and Round • Smoke on the Water • Sweet Child O' Mine • You Really Got Me.

VOL. 4 – POP/ROCK   00699571 / $12.95
Breakdown • Crazy Little Thing Called Love • Hit Me with Your Best Shot • I Want You to Want Me • Lights • R.O.C.K. in the U.S.A. • Summer of '69 • What I Like About You.

VOL. 5 – MODERN ROCK   00699574 / $12.95
Aerials • Alive • Bother • Chop Suey! • Control • Last Resort • Take a Look Around (Theme from *M:I-2*) • Wish You Were Here.

VOL. 6 – '90S ROCK   00699572 / $12.95
Are You Gonna Go My Way • Come Out and Play • I'll Stick Around • Know Your Enemy • Man in the Box • Outshined • Smells Like Teen Spirit • Under the Bridge.

VOL. 7 – BLUES GUITAR   00699575 / $12.95
All Your Love (I Miss Loving) • Born Under a Bad Sign • Hide Away • I'm Tore Down • I'm Your Hoochie Coochie Man • Pride and Joy • Sweet Home Chicago • The Thrill Is Gone.

VOL. 8 – ROCK   00699585 / $12.95
All Right Now • Black Magic Woman • Get Back • Hey Joe • Layla • Love Me Two Times • Won't Get Fooled Again • You Really Got Me.

VOL. 9 – PUNK ROCK   00699576 / $12.95
All the Small Things • Fat Lip • Flavor of the Weak • I Feel So • Lifestyles of the Rich and Famous • Say It Ain't So • Self Esteem • (So) Tired of Waiting for You.

VOL. 10 – ACOUSTIC   00699586 / $12.95
Here Comes the Sun • Landslide • The Magic Bus • Norwegian Wood (This Bird Has Flown) • Pink Houses • Space Oddity • Tangled Up in Blue • Tears in Heaven.

VOL. 11 – EARLY ROCK   00699579 / $12.95
Fun, Fun, Fun • Hound Dog • Louie, Louie • No Particular Place to Go • Oh, Pretty Woman • Rock Around the Clock • Under the Boardwalk • Wild Thing.

VOL. 12 – POP/ROCK   00699587 / $12.95
867-5309/Jenny • Every Breath You Take • Money for Nothing • Rebel, Rebel • Run to You • Ticket to Ride • Wonderful Tonight • You Give Love a Bad Name.

VOL. 13 – FOLK ROCK   00699581 / $12.95
Annie's Song • Leaving on a Jet Plane • Suite: Judy Blue Eyes • This Land Is Your Land • Time in a Bottle • Turn! Turn! Turn! • You've Got a Friend • You've Got to Hide Your Love Away.

VOL. 14 – BLUES ROCK   00699582 / $14.95
Blue on Black • Crossfire • Cross Road Blues (Crossroads) • The House Is Rockin' • La Grange • Move It on Over • Roadhouse Blues • Statesboro Blues.

VOL. 15 – R&B   00699583 / $12.95
Ain't Too Proud to Beg • Brick House • Get Ready • I Can't Help Myself • I Got You (I Feel Good) • I Heard It Through the Grapevine • My Girl • Shining Star.

VOL. 16 – JAZZ   00699584 / $12.95
All Blues • Bluesette • Footprints • How Insensitive • Misty • Satin Doll • Stella by Starlight • Tenor Madness.

VOL. 17 – COUNTRY   00699588 / $12.95
Amie • Boot Scootin' Boogie • Chattahoochee • Folsom Prison Blues • Friends in Low Places • Forever and Ever, Amen • T-R-O-U-B-L-E • Workin' Man Blues.

VOL. 18 – ACOUSTIC ROCK   00699577 / $14.95
About a Girl • Breaking the Girl • Drive • Iris • More Than Words • Patience • Silent Lucidity • 3 AM.

VOL. 19 – SOUL   00699578 / $12.95
Get Up (I Feel Like Being) a Sex Machine • Green Onions • In the Midnight Hour • Knock on Wood • Mustang Sally • Respect • (Sittin' On) the Dock of the Bay • Soul Man.

VOL. 20 – ROCKABILLY   00699580 / $12.95
Be-Bop-A-Lula • Blue Suede Shoes • Hello Mary Lou • Little Sister • Mystery Train • Rock This Town • Stray Cat Strut • That'll Be the Day.

VOL. 21 – YULETIDE   00699602 / $12.95
Angels We Have Heard on High • Away in a Manger • Deck the Hall • The First Noel • Go, Tell It on the Mountain • Jingle Bells • Joy to the World • O Little Town of Bethlehem.

VOL. 22 – CHRISTMAS   00699600 / $12.95
The Christmas Song (Chestnuts Roasting on an Open Fire) • Frosty the Snow Man • Happy Xmas (War Is Over) • Here Comes Santa Claus • Jingle-Bell Rock • Merry Christmas, Darling • Rudolph the Red-Nosed Reindeer • Silver Bells.

VOL. 23 – SURF   00699635 / $12.95
Let's Go Trippin' • Out of Limits • Penetration • Pipeline • Surf City • Surfin' U.S.A. • Walk Don't Run • The Wedge.

VOL. 24 – ERIC CLAPTON   00699649 / $14.95
Badge • Bell Bottom Blues • Change the World • Cocaine • Key to the Highway • Lay Down Sally • White Room • Wonderful Tonight.

VOL. 25 – LENNON & McCARTNEY   00699642 / $14.95
Back in the U.S.S.R. • Drive My Car • Get Back • A Hard Day's Night • I Feel Fine • Paperback Writer • Revolution • Ticket to Ride.

VOL. 26 – ELVIS PRESLEY   00699643 / $14.95
All Shook Up • Blue Suede Shoes • Don't Be Cruel • Heartbreak Hotel • Hound Dog • Jailhouse Rock • Little Sister • Mystery Train.

VOL. 27 – DAVID LEE ROTH   00699645 / $14.95
Ain't Talkin' 'Bout Love • Dance the Night Away • Just Like Paradise • A Lil' Ain't Enough • Panama • Runnin' with the Devil • Unchained • Yankee Rose.

VOL. 28 – GREG KOCH   00699646 / $14.95
Chief's Blues • Death of a Bassman • Dylan the Villain • The Grip • Holy Grail • Spank It • Tonus Diabolicus • Zoiks.

VOL. 29 – BOB SEGER   00699647 / $14.95
Against the Wind • Betty Lou's Gettin' Out Tonight • Hollywood Nights • Mainstreet • Night Moves • Old Time Rock & Roll • Rock and Roll Never Forgets • Still the Same.

VOL. 30 – KISS   00699644 / $14.95
Cold Gin • Detroit Rock City • Deuce • Firehouse • Heaven's on Fire • Love Gun • Rock and Roll All Nite • Shock Me.

VOL. 31 – CHRISTMAS HITS   00699652 / $12.95
Blue Christmas • Do You Hear What I Hear • Happy Holiday • I Saw Mommy Kissing Santa Claus • I'll Be Home for Christmas • Let It Snow! Let It Snow! Let It Snow! • Little Saint Nick • Snowfall.

VOL. 32 – THE OFFSPRING   00699653 / $14.95
Bad Habit • Come Out and Play • Gone Away • Gotta Get Away • Hit That • The Kids Aren't Alright • Pretty Fly (For a White Guy) • Self Esteem.

VOL. 33 – ACOUSTIC CLASSICS   00699656 / $12.95
Across the Universe • Babe, I'm Gonna Leave You • Crazy on You • Heart of Gold • Hotel California • I'd Love to Change the World • Thick As a Brick • Wanted Dead or Alive.

VOL. 34 – CLASSIC ROCK   00699658 / $12.95
Aqualung • Born to Be Wild • The Boys Are Back in Town • Brown Eyed Girl • Reeling in the Years • Rock'n Me • Rocky Mountain Way • Sweet Emotion.

VOL. 35 – HAIR METAL   00699660 / $12.95
Decadence Dance • Don't Treat Me Bad • Down Boys • Seventeen • Shake Me • Up All Night • Wait • Your Mama Don't Dance.

VOL. 36 – SOUTHERN ROCK   00699661 / $12.95
Can't You See • Flirtin' with Disaster • Hold on Loosely • Jessica • Mississippi Queen • Ramblin' Man • Sweet Home Alabama • What's Your Name.

VOL. 37 – ACOUSTIC METAL   00699662 / $12.95
Every Rose Has Its Thorn • Fly to the Angels • Hole Hearted • I'll Never Let You Go • Love Is on the Way • Love of a Lifetime • To Be with You • When the Children Cry.

VOL. 38 – BLUES   00699663 / $12.95
As the Years Go Passing By • Boom Boom • Cold Shot • Everyday I Have the Blues • Frosty • Further On up the Road • Killing Floor • Texas Flood.

VOL. 39 – '80S METAL   00699664 / $12.95
Bark at the Moon • Big City Nights • Breaking the Chains • Cult of Personality • Lay It Down • Living on a Prayer • Panama • Smokin' in the Boys Room.

VOL. 40 – INCUBUS   00699668 / $14.95
Are You In? • Drive • Megalomaniac • Nice to Know You • Pardon Me • Stellar • Talk Shows on Mute • Wish You Were Here.

VOL. 41 – ERIC CLAPTON   00699669 / $14.95
After Midnight • Can't Find My Way Home • Forever Man • I Shot the Sheriff • I'm Tore Down • Pretending • Running on Faith • Tears in Heaven.

VOL. 42 – CHART HITS   00699670 / $12.95
Are You Gonna Be My Girl • Heaven • Here Without You • I Believe in a Thing Called Love • Just Like You • Last Train Home • This Love • Until the Day I Die.

VOL. 43 – LYNYRD SKYNYRD   00699681 / $14.95
Don't Ask Me No Questions • Free Bird • Gimme Three Steps • I Know a Little • Saturday Night Special • Sweet Home Alabama • That Smell • You Got That Right.

Prices, contents, and availability subject to change without notice.

FOR MORE INFORMATION, SEE YOUR LOCAL MUSIC DEALER, OR WRITE TO:

HAL•LEONARD® CORPORATION
7777 W. BLUEMOUND RD. P.O. BOX 13819 MILWAUKEE, WI 53213

Visit Hal Leonard online at www.halleonard.com

0305